# A
# Picture
# History
# of
# BRITISH
# COLUMBIA

# A
# Picture
# History
# of
# BRITISH
# COLUMBIA

## George Woodcock

Hurtig Publishers
Edmonton

Hurtig Publishers Ltd.
10560 - 105 Street
Edmonton, Alberta

**Canadian Cataloguing in Publication Data**

Woodcock, George, 1912-
   A picture history of British Columbia

   ISBN 0-88830-185-5

   1. British Columbia — History — Pictorial works.
   I. Title.

FC3811.W66        971.1'0022'2        C80-091012-5
F1088.W66

Printed and bound in Canada

# Contents

# Introduction

A spectacular terrain filled with riches but hard to penetrate; an Indian culture more splendid than any other in North America; an arduous exploration by land and sea; a long-lasting frontier society dominated by fur and then gold; an economy always based on the ruthless exploitation of natural resources; a climate that has attracted people of many races, artists as well as miners, intellectuals as well as fishermen and loggers; all these factors have given British Columbian history a special cast, and they influence one's visual as well as one's conceptual view of the province's history.

Inevitably, the shapes of the land loom more boldly in the book that follows than they would do if it were not made around a province thought of — in Edward Blake's never-forgotten phrase — as "a sea of mountains", a province where life, for all its apparent sophistication in the twentieth century, of necessity remains close to the rock and the forest, to fresh water and salt chuck. Today, British Columbia is a highly urban society, at least in the distribution of its population, but the cities still hang on the edge of that massive hinterland, as they always have done. And so, in a peculiar way, this is the history of a land as well as of the people who have inhabited it, who have used its riches, who have tried to dominate it. If occasionally the people seem to be dwarfed by the scenery, that is in the nature of things British Columbian.

In terms of chronology, I have started with prehistory, since early man and his predecessors left signs on the rocks if they did not leave records; and, before the land was discovered, people in Europe had ideas about it which turned out to be wrong but are nevertheless part of history if not of geography. I have ended with the dawning of the 1980s.

I have not attempted to establish an exact correlation between text and illustrations. The narrative establishes autonomously the currents of regional history, the developments and issues and episodes of two centuries of recorded change. The illustrations are pictorial parallels that both complement and supplement the text. As in any combination of the visual and the written, the aim is mutual enrichment, the deepening of dimensions.

George Woodcock

Sailing up the coast of British Columbia the traveller sees little change from the days when Drake voyaged there four hundred years ago. The mountains still sweep forested to the salt water.

And the sun still percolates with difficulty through the rain forest.

# Before the White Men Brought History

British Columbia moved into history in two ways, by sea and by land. By sea it was first sighted in 1579, less than one hundred years after Columbus discovered the Americas. In that year Sir Francis Drake, sailing in the *Golden Hind*, skirted the Northwest Coast. He claimed the misty shoreline as New Albion in the name of Queen Elizabeth I, but he neither landed nor entered the channel that the Greek Apostolos Valerianos — commonly known as Juan de Fuca — claimed to have found in 1592, the strait that was believed to lead into the Strait of Anian, the mythical westward link with the Northwest Passage.

The coast Drake saw has changed little since he sailed beside it. Still the great rain forests tumble down the mountainsides into deep fjords, and still, here and there, stand the vast trees, survivors of first-growth cedars and Douglas firs that were saplings when King Alfred united the little Anglo-Saxon principalities into the realm of England in the ninth century A.D. But long before the Douglas firs evolved in the coastal rain forest, and even longer before man was seen there, the dinosaurs walked in the marshes and left the oldest footprints of living beings in British Columbia — to be unearthed by the geologists a million centuries afterwards.

These first-growth Douglas firs were a thousand years old when Captain Cook landed.

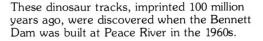

These dinosaur tracks, imprinted 100 million years ago, were discovered when the Bennett Dam was built at Peace River in the 1960s.

The first Indian arrived about 10,000 B.C. Most of his artifacts were perishable, but he left his record in stone carvings. Some showed the fish on which he depended for existence.

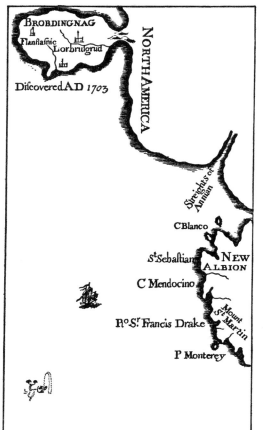

Brobdingnag, the land of the giants — imagined by Dean Swift as a peninsula projecting from what we now call British Columbia.

Man came late to British Columbia, as he did to all of the Americas, finding his way over the land bridge from Siberia that existed, up to the most recent ice age, where the Bering Strait now divides the Asian and the American continents. The earliest known British Columbian sites of human occupation, in the Fraser Canyon, seem to date from about twelve thousand years ago when the icefields of that last glacial era began to retreat and primitive hunters and fishermen could edge through the mountain passes and along the coast. All that those early men left were the great shell middens they deposited along the beaches, from which simple stone and bone artifacts have been removed, and the petroglyphs they carved on cliffs and boulders. Even the Indians of historical times did not know who had made the petroglyphs, but culturally these ancient men seem to have been not unlike the Coast Indian peoples whom the white men encountered when they finally landed at the end of the eighteenth century. Some of the petroglyphs recorded strange sea and land monsters, visions of whom may have come to young men during the trances of the spirit quest. Others simply depicted salmon and may have been part of a sympathetic magic aimed at ensuring that the supplies of essential food on which the coastal way of life depended arrived each year with the annual migration of the spawning fish.

For generations after Drake made his hurried reconnaissance, the coast of British Columbia remained such *terra incognita* that in 1726 Jonathan Swift, writing *Gulliver's Travels,* was able to place Brobdingnag, his fabulous kingdom of the giants, somewhere around the site of the Queen Charlotte Islands and very near the coastal mountains where, even today, Indian legends talk of a people of giants called the Sasquatch. As late as 1750, French map makers still showed the Strait of Juan de Fuca opening into a great inland sea, between the coast and the Rockies, which they named the Sea (or Bay) of the West.

Other petroglyphs showed — like this carving at Sproat Lake — the supernatural beings which primitive man believed he saw in visions.

This chart of "New Discoveries North of the Southern Sea, East of Kamchatka and West of New France", compiled by Phillippe Buache and Joseph Nicolas Delisle in 1750, shows Mexico and California exactly, but farther north it lapses into the conjectural, placing a great inland sea, reached by the mythical Strait of Anian, where most of British Columbia lies.

Masked Coast Indian chiefs danced in the prows of their elaborately carved canoes to welcome the first Spanish and English explorers, as shown in this later photograph by E. S. Curtis.

Captain James Cook.

# Explorers by Sea

All these mythical conceptions of the nature of the Pacific Northwest were changed in the last decades of the eighteenth century. Vitus Bering, a Dane voyaging eastward from Siberia in the employment of the Russian tsar, had already located and explored a great deal of Alaska in the summer of 1741, but by the time he died of scurvy that year, Bering had not voyaged as far south as the present British Columbian coast. Spaniards exploring northward from Mexico were the first Europeans to enter those waters. In 1774, on the *Santiago*, Juan Peréz sighted the Queen Charlotte Islands. He anchored off Vancouver Island near the entrance to Nootka Sound and encountered both the Haida and the Nootka Indians, with whom he traded for furs, but he did not land. Nor did Bruno de Hezeta who sailed the *Santiago* northward in 1775, accompanied by the *Sonora*, commanded by Juan Francisco de la Bodega y Quadra who proceeded up the coast as far as Alaska.

The first European explorer to land on what is now British Columbian territory was Captain James Cook. On March 29, 1778, during his third and last Pacific voyage, Cook sailed the *Discovery* and *Resolution* into Nootka Sound and established such excellent relations with the local Indians and their chief Maquinna that he named his anchorage Friendly Cove. He stayed almost a month, victualling his ships, brewing spruce beer as a preventive of scurvy, and caulking the *Resolution*. During this time Cook and his officers were the first Europeans to observe and record the prosperous and richly ceremonial way of life of the Coast Indian peoples. His artist John Webber portrayed the people living in their great houses of split cedar planks supported on elaborately carved posts; and Cook and his men gathered masks, rattles, and other artifacts (now in European museums) which showed a high level of sophistication and craftsmanship.

The crews of the *Discovery* and the *Resolution* also traded for furs and especially for the pelts of the sea otter. After Cook's death in Hawaii in 1779, his ships sailed home via Whampoa, and Chinese merchants eagerly bought the furs for use in mandarins' robes. When the journals of Cook's last voyage were published in 1784, the high prices paid for the sea otter pelts aroused the attention of English merchants, and from 1786 onwards a series of ships arrived at Nootka and began to trade up and down the coast in defiance of the Spanish claims to the region.

Among the many sea captains, English and later American, who arrived at this time, Captain John Meares made the greatest mark on history. Meares was not only the first European to acquire land in Canada west of the Rockies (by some kind of grant from Chief Maquinna); he also built there the *North West America,* the first craft other than an Indian canoe to be launched on the Coast.

In 1789, the year after the building of the *North West America,* Estevan José Martinez arrived with a small flotilla to assert Spain's right to Nootka by virtue of prior discovery. He declared Meares's title void, which it probably was, since Maquinna obviously had no conception of European ideas of property-owning when he let the English captain occupy the land. Martinez made matters worse by seizing the *North West America* and several other British ships sailing under Portuguese flags. He also built a fort and houses at Nootka — the first European settlement in the Pacific Northwest. In 1790,

Maquinna, the chief of the Nootka, welcomed Cook. A Spanish artist later drew his portrait.

The artist John Webber accompanied Cook on his expedition and painted the *Discovery* and the *Resolution* in Nootka Sound, surrounded by Indian canoes.

In his illustrations to the official narrative,
*Voyage to the Pacific Ocean,* 1784, Webber
gave European readers their first view of the
great houses of the coastal peoples.

But some of Webber's most interesting works
are vivid notations of people in action, like this
sketch of a Nootka woman weaving a
cedarbark blanket.

Meares took his grievance to the British House of Commons where he petitioned for redress, and at the threat of war the Spaniards backed down. Under the Nootka Sound Convention, Spain agreed to return the land seized from Meares and to compensate him. It was to implement the convention and to chart the coastline that Captain George Vancouver arrived on the Pacific Coast with the *Discovery* and the *Chatham* in April 1792.

Vancouver and Quadra — the Spanish commander — together circumnavigated and charted Vancouver Island and established that the strait named for Juan de Fuca did not lead to any great inland waterway and certainly not to the Northwest Passage; the Strait of Anian remained a myth. Vancouver left in 1794 without having settled the question of who possessed Nootka, but in 1795 the Spaniards finally withdrew and the British remained, for the time being at least, unchallenged on the Coast between California and Alaska.

Webber also drew the artifacts which Cook collected and which are now in great European museums.

Captain John Meares.

The launching of the *North West America* from the patch of land Meares thought he had bought from Maquinna.

The Spanish commander Martinez built this village on Nootka Sound after he seized the ships and property of Captain Meares.

The crisis resulting from Spanish actions at Nootka provoked political outcries in Britain, satirized in a cartoon by Samuel Collings that appeared in London during 1790 in *The Attic Miscellany: Or, Characteristic Mirror of Men and Things.*

Vancouver sailed a different *Discovery* from Cook's. Here it is aground in Queen Charlotte Sound with the *Chatham* in the background.

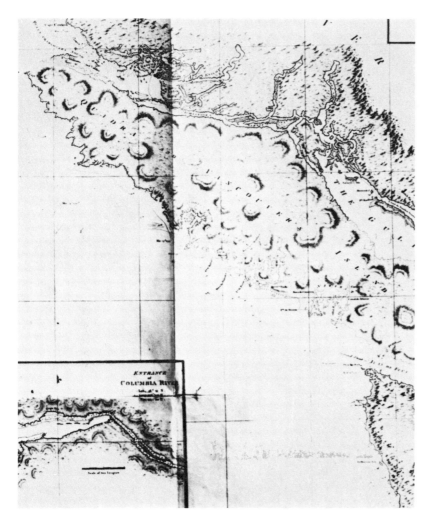

Captain George Vancouver.

Vancouver's *Voyage ... Round the World* (1798) included this map of the Pacific Coast; Vancouver Island bears its original name (Quadra and Vancouver Island) by which the English commander celebrated his friendship and harmonious co-operation with the Spanish commander Don Juan Francisco de la Bodega y Quadra.

Mackenzie and the other fur-trader explorers
travelled the dangerous rivers of British
Columbia by birchbark canoes, as in this
artist's impression of Chief Trader McDonald
descending the Fraser in 1828.

# Fur Traders by Land

On July 22, 1793, while Vancouver was charting the coast, the first European to cross Canada by land reached salt water at Dean Channel and heard from the Bella Bella Indians that he had just missed encountering a "large canoe" commanded by a man named "Macouba" whom they claimed had fired on them. The traveller was the fur trader Alexander Mackenzie, who had first set out to reach the Pacific in 1789 but had got to the Arctic Circle instead by way of the Mackenzie River. Mackenzie had started his second journey from the Peace River on May 9, 1793, and had made the difficult traverse of the Rocky Mountains and other ranges to the Bella Coola valley in about ten weeks.

Mackenzie was the forerunner of the fur traders who came by land. At first they were men of the North-West Company. In 1805 Simon Fraser crossed into what the North-westers called New Caledonia and founded Fort McLeod, the oldest surviving inland settlement in British Columbia. In 1806 he established Fort St. James, where Daniel Williams Harmon started the first farm west of the Rockies and grew barley and root crops.

The fur trade meant ever-extending exploration for new and productive fur-bearing regions and for routes by which to take the skins out of the country. Having founded Fort George in 1807, Fraser set out in 1808 on his great journey down the Fraser River to the Pacific. He was disappointed to reach the sea at Point Grey near the future site of Vancouver, for he had thought he was following the Columbia, whose mouth had been entered

Alexander Mackenzie, painted by Sir Thomas Lawrence in London, around 1800, after his journey to the Pacific.

Fort St. James, the most important North-West Company post in New Caledonia.

It was Simon Fraser who first opened the northern fur routes of British Columbia and later made the first exploration of the river named after him.

Daniel Williams Harmon, who at Fort St. James became the first British Columbian agriculturalist.

by Captain Robert Gray in 1792 and whose source David Thompson had recently discovered.

At first, the North-westers regarded the whole of the Pacific Coast between Russian Alaska and Spanish California as their legitimate trading territory. John Jacob Astor's American traders had established themselves at the mouth of the Columbia in 1811, but in 1813 the North-westers forced the surrender of Fort Astoria as a sideshow of the War of 1812, and after their company joined the Hudson's Bay Company in 1821 the united enterprise spread its posts along the coast. Fort Vancouver was established on the north side of the Columbia River in 1825, Fort Langley on the lower Fraser in 1827, and Fort Simpson at the mouth of the Skeena (where it served as a bastion to stop the Russians spreading south from Alaska) in 1831. The steamship *Beaver* arrived in 1835 to serve these coastal posts and trade up the intervening inlets.

The fur trade affected in many ways the life of the native peoples. Plentiful trade goods meant that the potlatches, or giving feasts, could be more lavish than ever; steel tools brought changes in the carving of totem poles, which were produced so abundantly that Haida and Kwakiutl villages became groves of carved wood; white sicknesses decimated peoples who had no natural resistance to them; firearms encouraged warfare. Into this transitional world, where old customs and new influences mingled in the last flowering of the traditional culture, the artist Paul Kane came in 1846 and recorded the passing way of life for posterity.

In the long run, the most important of all the new fur-trading posts was Fort Victoria, founded on the southern tip of Vancouver Island in 1843. By this time, American mountain men and immigrants had heavily penetrated the Oregon Territory, consisting of the present states of Washington and Oregon. American politicians, led by President Polk, were in an acquisitive mood and demanded the whole of the Pacific Northwest, from the Californian to the Alaskan border. They agitated under the slogan of "Fifty-four Forty or Fight" — 54°40' being the southernmost border of Alaska. The Hudson's Bay Company hoped to hold the line of the Columbia River, but in the Oregon boundary treaty (which was finally concluded in 1846 between Britain and the United States) the frontier was set at the 49th parallel with a slight diversion at the western end to include in British territory southern Vancouver Island and the vital port of Victoria.

For the time being, the Hudson's Bay Company retained its trading rights in the Oregon Territory, but it soon became evident that the company could not sustain the fur trade in a country so rapidly becoming settled. After feverish explorations, the routes of the fur brigades were diverted; instead of heading for the Columbia, they headed for the Fraser, and in 1849 the headquarters of the Columbia Department was shifted from vulnerable Fort Vancouver to Fort Victoria, where James Douglas ruled as chief factor.

This early photograph of Hell's Gate in the Fraser Canyon, with the Indian salmon drying on the rocks beside it, shows the fearsome terrain through which Fraser descended to the sea.

David Thompson, the other great fur-trader explorer, left no visual record of his travels, but Lieutenant Henry James Warre, on a British War Office mission in 1845, made this sketch of the source of the Columbia River which Thompson had discovered a generation before.

After Simon Fraser left the canyon and entered the lower valley, he encountered the immense wooden houses of the Coast Salish, like this one portrayed by Paul Kane in the 1840s. Fraser measured a house that was 1,500 feet long near the present site of Vancouver.

The steamship *Beaver,* which in 1835 revolutionized coastal trading.

The *Beaver* not only supplied the forts on the Pacific Coast; it also traded directly with Indian villages, and the transactions were recorded by the supercargoes in "skin-books" like this for 1839.

In a naive painting by an unknown artist, Fort Simpson is shown with the Tsimshian houses that sprang up around it; hostile canoes are arriving and exchanging musket fire with the local people.

A later Hudson's Bay ship, the *Otter*, is portrayed on the beach at Fort Simpson in the 1860s by George Staunton Brodie.

In 1845 Lieutenant Warre drew this early sketch of Fort Victoria.

James Douglas, who was given charge of the new fort at Victoria, was at Fort St. James in 1828 when Governor George Simpson of the Hudson's Bay Company arrived on his great trans-Canadian journey. The modern artist Adam Sherriff Scott envisaged their meeting in this painting.

"Leave well alone" was the policy of the fur traders in relation to Indian warfare, and Paul Kane in the 1840s witnessed bloody forays between peoples and villages, encouraged by the growing availability of arms. In two striking paintings Kane showed a raid on a village on the Olympic Peninsula (above) and a war party returning in triumph to the Indian village near Fort Victoria (below).

Paul Kane's painting of a Salish woman weaving a blanket is interesting for its incidental detail of Indian life. A woman in the background is spinning; the brow of the child on the cradle board is bound to shape his head; the white dog is of an extinct breed kept for their wool which was used in the blankets.

The unfortunate Governor Richard Blanshard.

## The Island Colony

After the Oregon boundary dispute was ended in 1846, the British government became aware of the need to establish some kind of authority on the Pacific Coast to counter further American claims, and in 1849 Vancouver Island was created a crown colony, the first regular outpost of government in North America west of Upper Canada. The Hudson's Bay Company was granted a licence of exclusive trade, on condition that it undertook settlement of the land. Richard Blanshard was appointed governor, but when he arrived he found that Chief Factor James Douglas wielded effective power, and since Douglas evaded co-operating with Blanshard, the unfortunate governor departed in frustration, and the Colonial Office accepted the fact that for the moment two authorities — the company and the crown — could not continue separate and side by side. James Douglas was appointed governor while retaining his post as chief factor for the company, and Fort Victoria became the centre of government as well as of trade.

The white population increased slowly. A few settlers arrived, scattering along the southern shore of the island, but they were not greatly encouraged by the company. Nevertheless, the goal of maximum self-sufficiency which Sir George Simpson, the Canadian head of the Hudson's Bay Company, had imposed on the Columbia Department led to the creation of

Fort Victoria, capital of the crown colony of Vancouver Island, with the *Beaver* anchored before it. The *Beaver*, a boat of 110 tons with a crew of twenty-six and five 9-pounder cannon, sailed round Cape Horn to the Pacific coast and was in service until her wreck on Prospect Point, Vancouver, in 1888.

an economy much more varied than that of the traditional fur trade. Already, before leaving the Oregon Territory, the company had founded a subsidiary, the Puget's Sound Agricultural Company. Under its auspices, farms were established at Craigflower and Colwood and other places in the southern parklands of Vancouver Island.

The lumber industry began with the first sawmill built at Victoria in 1848; by the following year it was exporting sawn wood to San Francisco. Commercial fishery began when barrels of salt salmon were prepared at Fort Langley for export to the Sandwich Islands, now called Hawaii. Coal was discovered in the northern part of Vancouver Island; miners were imported from England, and work began at Fort Rupert in 1849 and in 1854 at Colvile Town, which very soon became known by its modern name of Nanaimo. Thus, by 1850, the basic primary industries of British Columbia — logging, fishing, and mining — were already established.

James Douglas in official uniform as second governor of Vancouver Island.

John Muir arrived from Scotland in 1849 to work the mines at Fort Rupert. When his contract ended in 1852 he moved to Sooke on southwestern Vancouver Island, began cutting timber for piles, and in 1853 bought the land cleared by Captain Grant, the first settler.

Dr. J. S. Helmcken arrived at Fort Victoria as HBC surgeon in 1850 and married James Douglas's daughter in 1852, when he built one of the first houses outside the stockade. It still stands beside the provincial museum. The long low section is the original 1852 cottage, built of squared logs.

Early logging on Vancouver Island, recorded in the water colour of an artist, E. Sandy, of whom no biographical facts are known.

The only surviving building from the four farms of the Puget's Sound Agricultural Company near Victoria is Craigflower Manor, built in 1853 by Kenneth McKenzie, who ran Craigflower Farm as a kind of gentleman bailiff.

Fort Rupert was founded in 1849 when coal was discovered there. Lieutenant Mayne visited the post in 1860 and reported: "Fort Rupert is the newest and best station of the Hudson Bay Company I have seen, and the gardens are very nicely laid out."

Indian bands gathered around Fort Rupert, making it the most important Kwakiutl community. It was here that Franz Boas started his famous anthropological survey of the coastal culture.

Later coal was found at Nanaimo, which has remained a mining region ever since. It became a coaling station for the Royal Navy, and in 1859 Lieutenant Panter-Downes drew this sketch of the Hudson's Bay fort, the harbour installations, and a man-of-war lying off shore.

After years of isolated service in northern posts, John Tod arrived in British Columbia as chief factor of Fort Alexandria in 1823. Later he moved to Kamloops. In 1851 he retired to Victoria, where he became one of James Douglas's close advisers. Douglas appointed him a justice of the peace and a member of the Executive Council. He represented the conservative attitudes that critics of the company resented.

Tod lived almost ninety years and died in 1882. He married four wives, all of them Indian or Métis, the earlier ones without church ceremonies. The fourth and last, Sophia Tod, does not project in this portrait the spirit of her nickname "singing Lola".

## The Beginnings of Political Democracy

The political development of Vancouver Island was slow, largely because of its scanty white population: when Douglas assumed the governorship, there were less than a thousand in the whole territory that is now British Columbia. This small population was gathered mainly on the southern tip of Vancouver Island — in the fort and the little white log cottages outside its walls, and in the outlying farms, some of which, at Sooke, were thirty miles away. For a few years the colony remained a virtual autocracy, ruled by James Douglas with a minute three-man Executive Council and an appointed Legislative Council which consisted mainly of Hudson's Bay men, some of whom were linked to Douglas by marriage.

By 1855 criticism in Britain of the company's monopoly in Rupert's Land as well as on the Pacific Coast had become so strong that the British colonial secretary decided that a measure of democracy must be established on Vancouver Island. Douglas was somewhat disconcerted to receive instructions to

establish an elected legislative assembly. Because of the shortage of independent settlers, there were few people with the necessary qualifications for franchise — freehold property to the value of £300.

In the first election for the Legislative Assembly in 1856, only forty people were able to vote for the seven elected representatives, and only in Victoria did a real election take place. Elsewhere, the assemblymen were nominated without opposition. All of them were or had been employees of the company, but at least three had become bitter enemies of the governor, and even Douglas's son-in-law, the company's surgeon Dr. John Sebastian Helmcken who was chosen as Speaker, turned out to be a stickler for the privileges of this tiny parliament.

But there was little that the assembly — which had no building of its own and met in a smoky room at the fort — could do in the way of independent action, since its only source of revenue was from liquor licences and it did not have the power to borrow, while the company, its rival in authority, commanded large revenues not only from trade but also from selling land; even the royalties the company paid for the coal mines at Fort

Rupert and Nanaimo were administered directly by the governor. The assembly in its early stages was little more than a forum for public criticism of an administration in which the affairs of the company and those of the colony were mingled inextricably.

Yet whatever storms ruffled the island's political teacup, a strong social life developed in which everyone shared. There were annual horse races on the camas-blue grassland around Beacon Hill. There were balls and parties, to which the people picked their way through muddy streets. Sometimes the officers of naval survey ships graced these events with their presence, and there were return entertainments on the ships anchored in Esquimalt Harbour. A schoolmaster as well as a chaplain had arrived by 1849, and the first school was opened in 1851. For the daughters of those who considered themselves gentry there was even a Young Ladies' Academy. And all, young and old, joined in the picnics on the beaches and the riding parties among the open copses of garry oaks. If it had not been for the Indians who came down the coast to trade and camped on the seashore, it would have seemed an only slightly exotic version of the life of an early Victorian small town on the English coast.

Captain James Cooper, the harbour master of Victoria, was the unco-operative third member of the Executive Council and eventually became one of James Douglas's most fervent opponents.

Joseph Despard Pemberton arrived in 1851 and later became the colony's surveyor general. He laid out the first plan of the city of Victoria, surveyed the Pemberton area beyond the Coast Range, and founded a real estate firm that still operates in Victoria under his name.

In these fragile sketches of his dancing partners, Lieutenant Warre left a memento of the social pleasures of Fort Victoria.

Among the naval officers who contributed to the social life of early Victoria was Lieutenant Charles Mayne, who arrived in 1857 on the survey ship *Plumper* and left in 1861 when he was appointed commander. In 1862 Mayne published *Four Years in British Columbia and Vancouver Island*, with some of the first sketches of coastal waterways like Jervis Inlet (upper left) and Nootka Sound (lower left).

Within a few months of the arrival of the
*Commodore* in 1858, Victoria was
transformed from a sleepy fur-trading post to
an active small town with a busy harbour. In
this drawing from late in 1858 the miners'
tents can be seen among the new buildings
that arose around the shell of the stockade.

## The Gold Rush Transforms Victoria

On April 25, 1858, the existence of Vancouver Island as a remote
colony devoted to the fur trade came to an end. On Sunday
morning, as the Victorians were leaving church, an American
side-wheeler, the *Commodore*, moored in the harbour below the
fort and disgorged its freight of passengers. There were four hundred and fifty of them, as many as the population of the little
settlement, and they were mostly miners who had arrived too
late in California to make their fortunes. Gold had been found on
the North Thompson in 1857, and the company had provided the
Indians with iron spoons to dig the scales out of the cracks in the
bedrock. Shortly afterwards dust was found in the bars of the
Fraser River, and when the first consignment reached the assay
office in San Francisco, the new gold rush began; crowded
steamers sailed in rapid succession up the coast, and the
Victorians rejoiced at the sudden increase in trading possibilities,
not realizing how much it would change their surroundings and
their leisurely way of life.

Four hundred of the miners, having stocked up at the
Hudson's Bay store and the few independent shops, hurried
across the Gulf of Georgia in whatever craft were available and
made their way up the Fraser to the productive bars — Boston
Bar and Kanaka Bar and China Bar and a score of others. By the
end of the summer, twenty-five thousand men had passed

A slightly later panoramic view, by Hermann Otto Tiedemann, published in 1860, shows ships crowding the harbour and waiting outside in the roads.

The change from trading post to town meant that the fort interfered with development, and the company, intent on selling land, demolished the bastion — here shown in its last days — seventeen years after it was built; the rest of the fort was pulled down four years later.

In the streets on the site of the fort, the merchants from California erected first wooden and soon afterwards masonry structures in the San Francisco style, like this warehouse of an early merchant, which survives on Wharf Street.

Among the many groups of people who arrived in the first rush of 1858 were the free blacks from California who came north to find a place where they could be less persecuted. Samuel Booth, here shown in his masonic regalia, was one of the leading members of that community.

through Victoria into the Fraser Canyon, where they built their cabin settlements at the bars and rapidly exhausted the gold that could be obtained by primitive placer methods.

A street plan of Victoria had already been laid out by Joseph Despard Pemberton, the government surveyor who arrived in 1851, and now its outlines began to fill out with hastily erected wooden buildings; the first brick building, the Victoria Hotel, went up before the summer ended. In that season, 225 new structures were erected in six weeks. Two hundred of these were stores and saloons, most of them owned and operated by San Franciscans who realized that surer fortunes could be made by staying away from the gravel bars.

The hegemony of the Hudson's Bay Company had come to an end. Its trading monopoly was already terminated, and its physical presence began to recede. The northeast bastion of the fort was removed in 1860. The demolition of the whole structure was completed in 1864, giving way to the new streets, Wharf, Government, and Johnson, where the merchants set up their establishments. Doctors, officials, and sea captains began to build elegant clapboard houses, instead of log cabins, on the higher ground behind the harbour.

By 1866 there were six thousand people in Victoria served by eighty-five saloons and hundreds of stores. The population, hitherto almost entirely British, became cosmopolitan. There were native-born Americans, French, Germans, Italians. There was also a fair contingent of Chinese who settled around Fisgard Street, where Victoria's Chinatown still persists. A contingent of American blacks, tired of persecution by Southerners in California, arrived to seek the protection of the British flag; they formed the first volunteer military force in British Columbia.

Artists arrived from Canada and from Britain, and left their impressions of the changing scene. Victoria's gardens were, as they have remained, British, flourishing in the mild marine climate. The architecture, dominated by the merchant community, tended to be San Franciscan, though the new public buildings into which the Legislative Assembly moved in 1860 had an oriental flavour, with their pagoda roofs, and were immediately nicknamed "the Birdcages".

With the new arrivals of 1858 and 1859 the fourth estate came to Victoria. Two highly opinionated newspapers, the *Victoria Gazette* and the *British Colonist*, criticized the government of the colony and the economic power still wielded by the company, and demanded wider powers for the legislature. The editor of the *Colonist*, Amor De Cosmos, was to become not only the leading challenger of Governor Douglas but also a potent influence on the fate of Vancouver Island and its sister colony of British Columbia, which was founded in 1858.

To show their appreciation of the freedom they sought under the British flag, the blacks formed their own volunteer militia unit, the Victoria Pioneer Rifle Corps.

As Victoria grew under the impact of the gold rush, more elegant houses replaced the buildings of squared logs from the fur trade period. Captain Ella settled in Victoria in 1851 and became a local pilot. In the early 1860s he built his house on Fort Street from redwood imported from California.

Also in the early 1860s, this house was built at Point Ellice. In 1867 it was bought by Peter O'Reilly, one of the British Columbia gold commissioners.

As Victoria grew, artists gravitated there. William G. R. Hind, who came with the overlanders, painted the harbour round about 1864, showing the warehouses now clustering on the waterfront.

E. M. Richardson, an English painter who came west as a surveyor for American railways, rendered the same scene at the same time in a style reminiscent of Chinese painting.

The new colonial government buildings also showed a suggestion of Chinese influence in their pagodalike roofs. Opened in 1860, they were best known as "the Birdcages".

Amor De Cosmos, born in Nova Scotia as William Alexander Smith, arrived via the California goldfields in 1858 and immediately became a stringent critic of James Douglas and his undemocratic government.

# THE BRITISH COLONIST.

Vol. 2.     Victoria, Monday Morning, June 13th, 1859.     No. 1.

De Cosmos and his *British Colonist* became a focus for opposition.

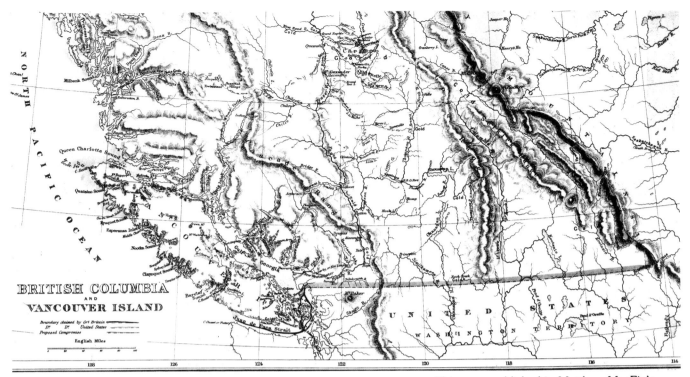

## The Second Colony

The rush to the Fraser River involved Governor James Douglas in an immediate crisis of jurisdiction. His rule officially extended only to Vancouver Island and the Queen Charlotte Islands (of which he had been appointed lieutenant governor during an earlier abortive gold rush in 1852). The mainland, still called New Caledonia, was without a government, though it was recognized as British territory under the Oregon boundary treaty of 1846; even before the *Commodore* arrived, Douglas was aware that a rush of miners — many of them American citizens — into the territory might, following the precedent of the Oregon Territory, become an excuse for American annexation if effective authority was not immediately established. Although he lacked any jurisdiction over the mainland, he had issued as early as December 1857 a proclamation that all gold mines in the Fraser and Thompson districts belonged to the British crown; and in January 1858 he announced a system of licences which every miner was obliged to obtain in Victoria before proceeding to the diggings.

While the Colonial Office in Westminster was pleased with Douglas's initiative, it recognized that his action was probably illegal, and the new colonial secretary (the novelist Lord Lytton) introduced legislation into the imperial parliament to create a government on the mainland. On August 2, 1858, the act received royal assent, and a new colony embracing the territory between the continental divide and the coast was created under the name of British Columbia, which Queen Victoria herself had chosen.

This map, published in Matthew MacFie's *Vancouver Island and British Columbia* in 1865, shows, in its repetition of the word "gold", the mainland areas into which prospectors were moving in the early 1860s.

A slightly romanticized prospector, with his primitive equipment, appears in a painting by William G. R. Hind, done round about 1864.

A more sophisticated way of dealing with placer gold was the rocker, shown in an engraving that illustrated MacFie's book.

The miners' camp at Fort Yale in the autumn of 1858, drawn by an artist for *Harper's Weekly*.

James Douglas was appointed governor of the new colony while retaining the governorship of Vancouver Island, which remained separate; but, to avoid further conflict of interests, he was forced to abandon his role as chief factor of the Hudson's Bay Company.

To help Douglas maintain law and order among the thousands of mostly armed miners flooding into the colony, a detachment of Royal Engineers, who would also be useful in public works, was sent out, while the screw-frigate Tribune reinforced the naval squadron. But equally effective was the appointment as judge of British Columbia of the flamboyant Matthew Baillie Begbie, who began a long career of horseback law-keeping in the scattered gold fields of the colony by ending — with a decisive show of authority backed by a few seamen and Royal Engineers — the minor insurrection at Hill's Bar, near Yale, led by the San Francisco desperado Ned McGowan. After "Ned McGowan's War", the threat of Californian lawlessness spreading to the Fraser River diggings no longer existed.

Very soon, the Royal Engineers were being used for more peaceful purposes. Douglas chose Fort Langley as the first

During the early gold rush days most of the traffic went via Yale, at the foot of the Fraser Canyon and head of navigation. From there the miners made their way upriver to the bars and beaches of the canyon. The steamship *William Irving* is here shown moored below the single street of the settlement, with the church built by the Royal Engineers in the background.

Matthew Baillie Begbie, judge of British Columbia and James Douglas's principal support in the mainland colony.

capital of British Columbia, and on November 19, 1858, in the main building of the Hudson's Bay Company's establishment, he was sworn in as governor by Judge Begbie. But when Colonel Richard Clement Moody was sent out to command the detachment of Royal Engineers and to act as chief commissioner of Lands and Works, he decided that the little settlement of Derby which was already springing up near Fort Langley was too vulnerable to American attack, and he chose instead a forested hillside on the northern shore of the Fraser. The woods were cleared, a new town was laid out, first called Queensborough, and on July 20, 1859, it was not only proclaimed capital of the colony under its new name of New Westminster (again chosen by Queen Victoria) but was also made the sole port of entry into British Columbia.

Here, until his term as governor of British Columbia ended in 1864, Douglas ruled — on the fairly rare occasions when he came over from Victoria — as autocratically as he had during his first years as governor of Vancouver Island. He had no legislative council or assembly. Moody and Begbie were his principal advisers, and he governed the vast province mainly through the ten gold commissioners — tough, wild-riding men, mostly Irish, who also acted as magistrates and were responsible for whatever simple civil government existed in the mining areas.

New Westminster — which, because of its more defensible site, eventually superseded Fort Langley as the colonial capital — is here shown at an early stage. On the left of the photograph is the house of Richard Clement Moody. On the far right is the house of Captain John Marshall Grant, who actually commanded the Royal Engineers in their road-building operations.

An early mission church among the stumps on the edge of New Westminster, illustrated in Mayne's *Four Years in British Columbia and Vancouver Island.*

An assay office for the colony of British Columbia was established in New Westminster. In 1862 it took on the functions of a mint and produced from Cariboo gold a $20 piece designed by Captain William Driscoll Gosset, treasurer of the colony.

The first ocean-going ship to sail up the Fraser to New Westminster, which sought to rival Victoria as the seaport of the West Coast; both ports eventually lost ground to Burrard Inlet, which became Vancouver.

This drawing of New Westminster was probably done shortly before British Columbia entered Confederation, for the plan laid out by Captain Grant was already being filled in with streets and houses which sent the woods retreating up the hillsides.

H.M.S. *Modeste* undergoes repairs at Fort Simpson in 1844.

# The Royal Navy and the Pig War

After the foundation of Fort Victoria, ships of the Royal Navy began to appear regularly on the north Pacific coast. They fulfilled three functions: to carry on the surveying that Captain Vancouver had started; to protect the small number of white people from possible attacks by the far more numerous Indians; and to show the flag and discourage foreign interference — which meant either Russian penetration from Alaska or American adventurers from the south.

In 1844, as the Oregon boundary crisis moved towards fever point, Her Majesty's sloop *Modeste* sailed to Fort Vancouver on the Columbia to show that Britain did not lightly abandon its claims there, and then proceeded to Fort Simpson on the Skeena so that the Russians would have no doubt that in that region the Hudson's Bay Company was acting under British protection. Until the dispute over the Oregon Territory was settled in 1846, other ships like the *Cormorant,* the *Fisgard,* and the *Pandora* (remembered in Victoria street names) sailed in the waters around Vancouver Island.

Naval commanders found the harbour at Esquimalt convenient, and when coal was discovered at Fort Rupert and later Nanaimo, this gave added reason to consider establishing a per-

H.M.S. *Plumper* arrived for survey work in 1857. This sketch by E. P. Bedwell appeared in the *Illustrated London News* in 1862.

49

The Fisgard lighthouse was built in 1859 to protect shipping entering Esquimalt Harbour. It was named after H.M.S. *Fisgard* which was stationed on the Pacific Coast between 1844 and 1847.

Rear-Admiral Sir Robert Lambert Baynes was commander-in-chief of the Pacific station between 1857 and 1860, the most sensitive years of the San Juan dispute.

During the San Juan crisis, cannon were installed near Victoria in case of American attack.

H.M.S. *Ganges,* launched at Bombay in 1821 and mounting eighty-four guns, was the flagship of Admiral Baynes.

manent naval base on southern Vancouver Island. Ships began to refit at Esquimalt; during the Crimean War hospital huts were located there, and lighthouses were built shortly afterwards. In 1862, considering the advantages of an establishment on British soil, the Admiralty decided to transfer the headquarters of the Royal Navy's Pacific station from Valparaiso to Esquimalt. The harbour remained an important British naval base until 1910 when, after the creation of a separate Canadian navy, it was handed over to the dominion.

The most dangerous local crisis in which the navy became involved was the dispute over the San Juan Islands, which lie south of the 49th parallel between the American mainland and southern Vancouver Island. The wording of the 1846 treaty regarding the maritime boundary was vague enough for both parties to claim the islands, and on the westernmost, San Juan, the Hudson's Bay Company set up a sheep station. The Americans countered by officially including the islands in the newly founded Washington Territory, and in 1859 the shooting of a Hudson's Bay Company's pig by an American settler pushed the confrontation to the edge of war.

As charges and countercharges of violated sovereignty were exchanged, the Americans established a military force on San Juan Island, and Governor Douglas proposed to counter in kind. It was the restraint of Rear-Admiral Baynes, then in charge of

H.M.S. *Tribune*, a screw-frigate of thirty-one guns, was called to the Pacific Coast at the height of the Fraser Valley rush and arrived in 1859, in time to show the flag off the San Juan Islands.

the Pacific station, that kept the peace until a compromise was worked out, and General Winfield Scott was sent from Washington to ensure that the islands were occupied by equal forces of the two parties until the dispute over ownership was solved.

Douglas had seen the incident as an opportunity to recover as British territory the land that the Hudson's Bay Company had lost in 1846; as late as 1861 he was urging the British government to take advantage of American attention being distracted by the Civil War and send an expedition to occupy Puget Sound and establish a permanent frontier on the Columbia. Douglas was reprimanded and, to his chagrin, ordered to maintain a strict neutrality towards both sides in the Civil War.

Even without Douglas's impetuosity, the 1860s was a period of tension in which a large naval force, sometimes with as many as sixteen warships and never with less than twelve, was centred on the new base at Esquimalt. The Civil War ended in 1865 with a revival of American expansionist aggressiveness. The confederation of Canada in 1867 angered many American leaders, who talked once again of annexing British Columbia; the purchase of Alaska by the United States in 1867 made the situation even more precarious, while the continuing disagreement over the San Juan Islands remained a local irritant.

Finally, in the Washington Treaty of 1871, the outstanding differences between the British and the Americans were worked out, and the fate of the San Juan Islands, on which neither side was willing to give way, was left for arbitration by Kaiser William I of Germany. In 1872 the Kaiser decided in favour of the Americans, and vessels of the Royal Navy withdrew the British forces from San Juan Island. From this time onwards there was no physical threat by the Americans to British Columbia, now a part of the Dominion of Canada.

Surveying and facing up to the Americans were not the only duties of the Royal Navy on the Pacific Coast. Sometimes the navy was used against Indians who attempted to plunder coastal ships; in 1864 boats from the *Devastation* and the *Sutlej* attacked native villages in Clayoquot Sound with rockets.

The Flying Squadron of the Pacific command, making a show of force in 1871, anchors in Esquimalt Harbour. From left to right, the *Liverpool* (front), *Endymion,* (behind), *Liffey, Zealous, Phoebe, Charybdis.*

H.M.S. *Zealous*, the first ironclad on the
Pacific Coast, was flagship from 1867 to 1872.

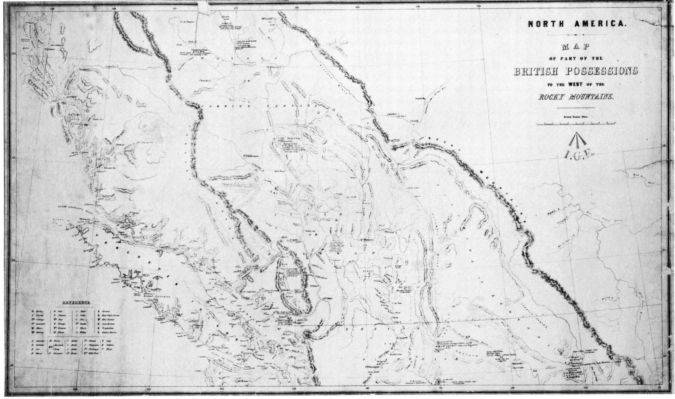

British anxiety over the San Juan crisis led the
War Department in 1869 to prepare this map
of British Columbia. With a thoroughness
characteristic of nineteenth-century
topographers, its references note wildlife and
local vegetation.

# The Road to Cariboo

By 1859 the bars of the lower Fraser were already worked out and the gold miners left them to the Chinese, who were willing to toil for small takings, and began to move northward, following dangerous footpaths along the Fraser Canyon to Boston Bar and on to Lytton and Lillooet. There was an alternative route up the Harrison River to the little settlement of Douglas at the head of Harrison Lake and thence by a trail the miners themselves had made via Seton and Anderson lakes to Lillooet, which became a halting place for miners setting out on prospecting journeys farther up the Fraser River.

In 1860 Edgar Dewdney established the Dewdney Trail from Hope to the Similkameen River, following much the same route as the present Hope-Princeton Highway, and later the Royal Engineers under Captain J. M. Grant entered the scene, widening both the Douglas and the Dewdney trails into good wagon roads, beside which primitive inns were built to shelter travellers and refresh their animals. There was a certain political intent in building these roads, and particularly the Dewdney Trail, which it was hoped would prevent the economy of the border districts from being dominated by American merchants in Washington Territory.

By 1860 the northward flow of miners was stimulated by rich

The first miners to penetrate beyond the Fraser Valley made their own way through the rough terrain, like these wayfarers portrayed by William G. R. Hind.

Until roads were built, most of the traffic to the mines was by expensive pack trains.

One of the earliest usable ways beyond the lower Fraser Valley was the Dewdney Trail, following roughly the route of the present Hope-Princeton Highway to Similkameen. It was constructed by Edgar Dewdney, who later became lieutenant governor of the North-West Territories and eventually of British Columbia.

finds of gold at Horsefly east of Lac La Hache and on the Quesnel River. The miners had reached the verge of the famous Cariboo country. Later that summer "Doc" Keithley discovered the creek that bears his name, and the miners stampeded there and to Antler Creek. During the following winter "Dutch" William Dietz crossed Bald Mountain from Keithley Creek and gave his name to Williams Creek, where the deep gravels gave the richest yields of all. By 1861 almost equally productive veins had been found in the neighbouring Lightning and Lowhee creeks, and by 1862 an even bigger stampede than the original Fraser River rush was on. Tens of thousands of men — and not a few women — were making their way to the Cariboo from Canada, from the United States, and this time in large numbers from Britain and Europe. In the spring of that year alone, five thousand miners made their way north by whatever trails existed, and Governor Douglas was confirmed in his view of the need for a Great North Road that would take the most direct way, through the Fraser Canyon.

Douglas decided to construct the Cariboo Road — as it was eventually named — by a combination of military and civilian labour. In May 1862, Captain Grant began work on the difficult section from Yale to Boston Bar and also on a section along the Thompson River near Spence's Bridge, in both of which blasting of rock faces and the construction of cribbing to support the road would be needed. The rest of the road was to be built by civilian contractors, one of whom was Joseph W. Trutch, later to play a considerable role in the entry of British Columbia into Confederation. By 1863 the stage coaches were running between Yale and Soda Creek, far above the Fraser Canyon, where the passengers proceeded by steamer to Quesnel; from there Captain Grant had cut a trail to Williams Creek by way of Cottonwood River. Within the next two years, by the autumn of 1865, the highway link had been made between Soda Creek and Quesnel, and the trail from Quesnel to Williams Creek had been turned into a wagon road along which the stage coaches could ride to Barkerville and Richfield, the twin centres of the Cariboo gold field.

Douglas, at the head of Harrison Lake, the beginning of the trail via Anderson and Seton lakes.

Avoiding the canyon, the Douglas Trail reached the upper Fraser at Lillooet, which W. S. Hatton drew in 1864.

From Lillooet, a steep serpentine trail ran to the level of 4,000 feet over Pavilion Mountain. Known as the "Rattlesnake Grade", it was portrayed with some exaggeration by Viscount Milton and Dr. Cheadle in their narrative *The North-West Passage by Land*, 1865.

When it was finally decided to build the Cariboo Road, much of it was done by contractors, but the most difficult stretches were built by the Royal Engineers, here imaginatively portrayed by the modern artist Rex Woods.

17-Mile Bluff, at the lower end of the Cariboo Road, between Yale and Spuzzum, showing the method of construction along the cliffsides.

At Great Bluff, 88 miles north of Yale, a way had to be blasted through the rock walls.

The Alexandra Bridge was built by Joseph W. Trutch, then a private contractor. He later became commissioner for public works and eventually the first lieutenant governor of British Columbia. The painting is by E. T. Coleman.

59

Hostelries sprang up along the Cariboo Road, ranging from simple road houses to larger establishments like the Clinton Hotel. On the balcony in this early photograph is F. J. Barnard (proprietor of the stage coaches standing outside the hotel) and his wife.

A freight wagon makes its way through woodland on the Cariboo Road.

In the early days, before the road was completed to the heart of the Cariboo, passengers and freight were trans-shipped at Soda Creek to stern-wheelers which took them to Quesnel Forks, painted by Frederick Whymper in 1864. From there a trail went inland via Cottonwood House to Barkerville.

# The Overlanders

Not all the people who set off for the Cariboo in the enthusiastic year of 1862 went by way of Governor Douglas's new roads from the Pacific coast. Others decided to find their way overland — and literally so, for instead of following the canoe paths of the fur traders, they chose to travel as far as possible across the open prairies and then on foot through the mountain passes. They started from various places in Upper and Lower Canada, gathering at St. Paul in the United States. Here, 160 of them embarked on a steamer for Fort Garry. By the time they reached this point, some had already decided the enterprise was too arduous, but 135 remained to set out with 97 Red River carts and 110 horses and oxen.

Like the Métis hunters of the prairies, the overlanders held an election to choose their leader — Captain Thomas R. McMicking, who was to be assisted by a council of thirteen. Among the group who set out across the prairies (following a route already being canvassed by promoters of the idea of a wagon road and telegraph between Upper Canada and the Pacific) were the artist William G. R. Hind and one woman, Catherine Schubert, who, with her three children, was accompanying her husband. The wagon train was half a mile long as it straggled over the prairies, and every night the overlanders would imitate the custom of the Métis, forming their carts into a triangle within which they camped for fear of raids by Indians.

By July 21 the overlanders had reached Fort Edmonton. Here some of them dropped out, but 125 set out on July 29 on the most arduous part of their journey, this time accompanied by 150 pack animals. They made a slow way through the Rockies and did not reach Tête Jaune Cache until August 27, when almost all their food was gone. Here they decided to divide into two groups. The larger group, more than a hundred men, built five large rafts to carry themselves and what stock had survived

Thomas McMicking of Queenston was elected captain of the overlanders when they left White Horse Plains outside Fort Garry for British Columbia. Like so many overlanders, he never mined gold. He became sheriff of New Westminster and, having survived the rigours of the overland journey, was drowned in the Fraser in 1886 when he vainly attempted to save his son.

The painter William G. R. Hind was one of the overlanders, and among the many sketches he made was this one of the prospective miners leaving Fort Garry with their ox-drawn Red River carts.

Hind's sketch of two overlanders, Jones and Carpenter, playing cards in their tent, evokes the strangest tragedy of the journey. Carpenter was drowned trying to take a canoe through the Grand Canyon of the Fraser above Fort George. He had been seen writing in a notebook which he left in a jacket laid beside the river when he got into the canoe. When his companions opened the diary after his death, they found he had written: "Arrived at Grand Canyon; ran the rapids and was drowned."

Catherine, wife of Francis Augustus Schubert, was the only woman among the overlanders; on October 14, 1862, the day after arriving at Kamloops, she gave birth to a daughter, Rose, the first white child born in interior British Columbia. She lived on for more than fifty years, dying in 1918.

Hind's drawing of the overlanders at the foot of the Rockies.

through the rapids and canyons of the Fraser. One man was drowned, but the rest reached Quesnel on September 11.

The smaller group of twenty people, including Mrs. Schubert and her family, set out overland to Fort Kamloops, and after extraordinary hardships made their way through this rugged terrain, reached the North Thompson, and came to Kamloops on October 13. On the next day Mrs. Schubert was delivered of a daughter, Rose, the first white child to be born in the interior of British Columbia.

The epic journey of the overlanders was repeated almost as arduously by the first avowed tourists to make their way across Canada, Viscount Milton and Dr. Cheadle, who travelled more lightly than the overlanders and thus were often able to avail themselves of traditional ways of water transport. They spent the summer of 1863 crossing the continent and reached the Cariboo gold field in October. Having no fortune to seek, they were able to observe more freely, and their lively book *The North-West Passage by Land* did a great deal to arouse interest in the idea of linking British Columbia with Canada when it appeared in 1865.

Milton and Cheadle travelled more quickly
and a shade more comfortably than the
overlanders, but the illustrations of their
*North-West Passage by Land* suggest the
rigours of roadless journeys through the wild
interior. This is entitled "Mr. O'B triumphantly
crosses the river".

Even at journey's end, when roads and human
habitations were reached, conditions of travel
were only slightly less primitive, as is shown
by these sketches of the roadhouses where
Milton and Cheadle stayed.

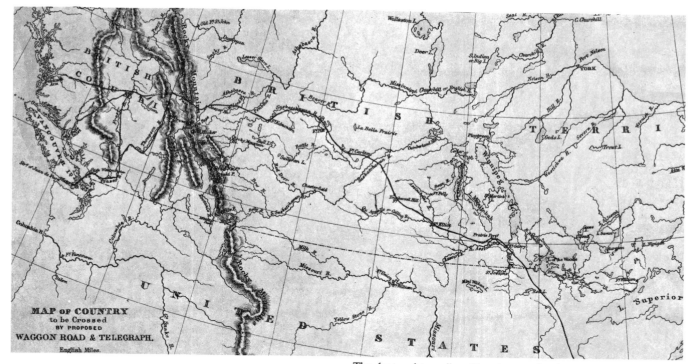

MAP of COUNTRY
to be Crossed
BY PROPOSED
WAGGON ROAD & TELEGRAPH.

English Miles.

The feats of travellers like the overlanders and Milton and Cheadle inspired those concerned with communications between British Columbia and Canada. Before the idea of a railway was accepted, several schemes were devised for wagon roads across the continent, along which telegraph lines would be erected. This map of such a scheme appeared in 1865 in MacFie's *Vancouver Island and British Columbia*.

In *The Wild North Land* a later overlander, Captain William Francis Butler, vividly represented the adventures of travel in the Rockies in prints like "Running Stern Foremost the Black Canyon" and "Cutting up the Moose".

The wheel and flume that worked the pump on the Davis claim at Williams Creek.

## Gold Rush Metropolis

On every creek in the Cariboo, instant towns sprang up as soon as rich finds were made. Miners' cabins would be perched on the hillsides above the claims; there would be shops and hotels and saloons and gambling houses along a rough lane of a main street; the gold commissioner and the postmaster would arrive, and finally Judge Begbie himself, sometimes to hold court on horseback in his wig and crimson robes. But in most cases the gold dust did not meet expectations, the miners departed, and the bush began to sprout again among the falling houses of what quickly became ghost towns.

The one gold-mining settlement that did continue to prosper for many years, and even today survives as an antiquarian curiosity, was that trio of towns which sprang up beside Williams Creek: Richfield, and then Barkerville, and finally Camerontown. Richfield — where a permanent courthouse was built for Begbie's cases to be heard and a jail to hold his prisoners — became the centre of government. Camerontown was named after the famous Cariboo Cameron who made and lost one of the great fortunes of the region. He is best known for having brought his wife to the diggings and, when she died there, having taken her out for burial in Scotland, preserved in a lead coffin filled with whisky. Not inappropriately, Camerontown was the site of the cemetery where the gold miners were buried. But it was

Barkerville, named after the Cornishman Billy Barker and situated between Richfield and Camerontown, that became the real centre of life on Williams Creek.

It is said, probably truly, that for a time Barkerville was the most populous community in North America west of Chicago. Estimates of the number of people who lived there vary, but the town probably had at least ten thousand inhabitants when Victoria had no more than six thousand, and it was much larger than New Westminster, then the capital of British Columbia.

In fact, Barkerville looked much more like a rough mountain village than a town in the real sense. A narrow street, usually deep in mud, followed a straggling way along the valley bottom, with high sidewalks behind which stood buildings of whipsawn lumber that housed hotels and banks, laundries and barber shops, bakeries and groceries, banks and blacksmith shops. There was a theatre, visited by touring companies from San Francisco, and a twice-weekly newspaper, the *Cariboo Sentinel*. There was even a resident poet, James Anderson, whose *Sawney's Letters* were published as well as written in Barkerville; and the terpsichorean art was somewhat inelegantly served by the Hurdy Gurdies, German girls dressed in vaguely Tyrolean garb who served as dancing partners for the miners. As "Sawney" put it:

> Bonnie are the hurdies, O!
> The German hurdy-gurdies, O!
> The daftest hour that e'er I spent
> Was dancin' wi' the hurdies O!

The Cornish miner Billy Barker became a seaman and in 1858 deserted his ship to join the Fraser Valley gold rush. On August 21, 1862, at the bottom of a shaft 42 feet deep, Barker hit pay dirt, and he and his partners brought out gold valued at $600,000. Barkerville was named after him, but in spite of his fame he lost his fortune, failed to make another, and died a pauper in 1894.

Camerontown may have been smaller and less durable than Barkerville, but Cariboo Cameron's claim was richer even than Barker's.

For those of more serious mind, Barkerville provided a library and several churches, while, as in most gold-mining settlements, there was a Chinatown and a Chinese masonic hall.

In 1868 Barkerville was wiped out by a fire that destroyed the whole town in an hour and twenty minutes. The damage — enormous in those days — was estimated at $690,000 in property and $700,000 in goods. The rebuilding of the town commenced immediately, and by the time Governor Musgrave visited it a year later, Barkerville gave such an impression of prosperous gaiety that it was hard to tell there had ever been a conflagration. Nevertheless, it was the beginning of the end for Barkerville. Mining there had always been difficult because deep shafts had to be sunk to bedrock, and it quickly ceased to be an occupation

As the more accessible gold was worked out, more expensive methods like hydraulic mining were used, which meant the end of the small groups of miners working their own claims and the advent of well-capitalized mining companies.

The main street of Barkerville before the fire of September 1868.

for individual placer miners. Soon most miners were employees of the syndicates who had the capital to sink the shafts, and as the gold dwindled and newer forms of mining like hydraulic sluicing and the use of dredges in the valley bottom came into vogue, the population steadily diminished and the town gradually shrank. Today, there are only a few buildings left even of the "new" Barkerville of 1868-69, and these are preserved because they are tourist attractions.

During the 1860s almost $20 million in gold was reported to have been dug in Williams Creek and the tributary gulches, but much gold was also taken out of the area without being recorded. It was the largest Canadian gold rush before the Klondike stampede nearly forty years later.

One of the hostelries on Barkerville's straggling main street.

The Wake-up-Jake Saloon and J. H. Todd's general store, decorated for a Christmas before the great fire.

W. D. Moses, the Barkerville barber, came to Victoria with the first batch of black immigrants in 1858. He became a famous citizen of Barkerville and once, with some smart deduction, solved a local murder mystery. His advertisement appeared in the *Cariboo Sentinel*, Barkerville's local newspaper.

The Richfield branch of the Bank of British Columbia, one of several banks that appeared and disappeared in response to the gold rush. It has no link, except by name, with the present Bank of British Columbia, which was founded in 1967.

The Cariboo Gold Escort was established by the British Columbia government to take gold from the Cariboo to New Westminster, but most miners preferred to make their own arrangements, distrusting the escort only a little less than the potential bandits.

Built shortly after the fire of 1868, the Anglican church is one of the few surviving buildings of old Barkerville.

In this drawing of Richfield, made round about 1863, the courthouse where Judge Begbie presided is indicated by the Red Ensign posted beside it.

The pattern of flumes at Richfield, c. 1865.

The decaying jail at Richfield and, beside it, a corner of the courthouse.

Barnard's Express on the way to Barkerville.

A playbill for a San Francisco company performing at the Theatre Royal in Barkerville, round about 1868.

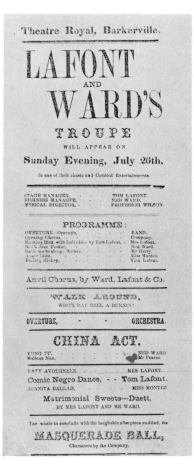

# The United Colony

An era on the Pacific Coast came to an end with the withdrawal of James Douglas from the pre-eminence he had enjoyed since Victoria was founded in 1843. In 1863, with his term as governor of Vancouver Island drawing to a close, he was knighted for his services to the crown, and in 1864 he retired from the governorship both of Vancouver Island and of British Columbia.

From this point, for a brief two years, the colonies were administered by separate governors. Arthur Edward Kennedy, a martinet who had successively been governor of Gambia, Sierra Leone, and Western Australia, ruled in Victoria. Frederick Seymour, who had been lieutenant governor of British Honduras, ruled in New Westminster. Although, unlike Douglas, both men were career colonial servants, Seymour was popular on the mainland, to whose expansive frontier cast of mind his easy-going nature responded, while Kennedy's strict aloofness made him unpopular in Victoria, where even a close friend remarked that in the governor's presence "it was not easy for me, his inoffensive personal friend, waiting the announcement of dinner, to rid myself from a suspicion that I was in the guardroom, and that I deserved it."

In part, the difference between the achievements of the two governors was due to the different political systems in which they worked. Kennedy inherited the elected Legislative Assembly of Vancouver Island and became involved in bitter disputes over questions of finance and parliamentary privilege with an assembly dominated by De Cosmos, the fiery democrat, and Helmcken, the stickler for parliamentary forms. At one period the assembly went so far as to refuse a grant for the governor's residence, and this seemed excessive even to the people of Victoria (incorporated as a city in 1862) who held a public meeting to express their indignation at this insult to the Queen's representative.

On the mainland, when Sir James Douglas's autocratic form of government came to be modified in 1864, the legislative body did not take the form of an elected assembly but of a legislative council in which only five members were elected, while ten were appointed, which gave the officials and the stipendiary magistrates a control over the way colonial affairs were regulated. Governor Seymour dealt smoothly with his council, finding support where he needed it in the appointed majority and also, by his congenial ways — he liked gambling and high living — gathering a following among the merchants of New Westminster and the miners of Cariboo.

The period after Douglas's retirement was a time of recession, as the mining booms diminished and population dribbled away from both Victoria and the communities of the mainland. Economic problems and the difficulties with Governor Kennedy led the popular leaders in Victoria to agitate for the union of the two colonies, and they were finally willing to accept any terms on

Sir Arthur Edward Kennedy, the third and last governor of Vancouver Island.

Frederick Seymour, who succeeded Sir James Douglas as governor of British Columbia, became governor of the united colony.

Castle Cary, also called Cary Folly, was built by George Hunter Cary, who arrived in Victoria in 1859 and became attorney general of Vancouver Island and also — in absentia — of British Columbia. In 1864, when Cary departed for England, Governor Kennedy bought the folly for $40,000 and made it into Government House. The transaction was one of the many causes of contention between Kennedy and his assembly.

When Victoria received its city charter in 1862, the butcher Thomas Harris became first mayor. He weighed 300 pounds and his chair collapsed under him at the first council meeting. Although he was the friend of Amor De Cosmos, Harris organized the movement to protest against the assembly's refusal to grant Governor Kennedy funds for a residence.

which the imperial government might decree amalgamation. Here they had reckoned without the duplicity of Governor Seymour who, despite his democratic manners, had no love for the democratic practices of the Vancouver Island assembly. Seymour went to England at the end of 1865 to advise the colonial secretary on the political structure of the united colony, of which he would become governor, and when the terms of union were made known in September 1866, it was revealed that the Vancouver Islanders would lose their elected assembly; the new colony, to be named British Columbia, would be ruled by an enlarged legislative council, in which the nine elected members — four from the island and five from the mainland — would be more than balanced by the six government officers and the seven stipendiary magistrates who sat as appointed representatives. De Cosmos allied himself, at least temporarily, with the more democratically inclined mainland representatives, John Robson of New Westminster (editor of the *British Columbian*) and George Anthony Walkem, surveyor, lawyer, and gifted Sunday painter, who represented Cariboo. All of them eventually became premiers of British Columbia.

Victoria was adversely affected in more than one way by the union of the colonies. It lost its privileges as a free port, and it was replaced as colonial capital by the much more rustic centre of New Westminster. From the beginning, conscious that the roots of his influence lay on the island, Amor De Cosmos advocated a return to Victoria. It was the first of many occasions on which his alliance with Robson was strained, for the editor of the *Columbian* felt that the economic strength of the mainland justified a mainland capital. Finally, the preference of the government officials for the comforts of residence in Victoria settled the issue when a free vote was held. In March 1868 — by fourteen to five — the council elected to depart for Victoria, where it took over the old assembly chamber in the Birdcages and prepared to debate the logical step following on colonial union — confederation with the recently created Dominion of Canada.

Government House in New Westminster, sketched in 1870 by Lady Musgrave, was actually the house of Colonel Moody, built for himself a decade before.

An incomplete group portrait of the first Legislative Council of British Columbia, on the stairs of the colonial government building in 1864. They are, from left, Henry Holbrook, George A. Walkem (later a premier of British Columbia), Chartres Brew, H. M. Ball, A. N. Birch, C. W. Franks, Peter O'Reilly, Walter Moberley, J. A. R. Horner, Charles Good (who by some photographic accident appears like a materializing apparition), and H. P. P. Crease, the attorney general.

John Robson, editor of the *British Columbian* and leader of the tiny democratic minority in the Legislative Council.

A street in Victoria in 1868, when it became capital of British Columbia.

# Canada on the Pacific

Long before John A. Macdonald led the Canadian delegates to the historic Charlottetown Conference of 1864 and set the process of Confederation into motion, the idea of a continent-wide union of the British possessions was being discussed on the Pacific Coast. As early as 1860 Amor de Cosmos in the *Colonist* had celebrated the Prince of Wales's visit to Canada with a call for the initiation of "a British North American policy to put an end to disjointed provinces", and after 1863, when he entered the Vancouver Island assembly, he advocated North American union as well as the union of the two Pacific colonies.

Later, in 1866, as it became evident that negotiations between the Canadas and the Atlantic Colonies were leading to some kind of confederation, De Cosmos — with the rather unexpected support of Dr. Helmcken — pressed Governor Seymour in the British Columbia Legislative Council to ask the colonial secretary that any imperial act confederating the eastern colonies should provide for the eventual inclusion of British Columbia.

Seymour did not favour Confederation, and procrastinated, while De Cosmos went east to consult with the Canadians who

Yale in 1868, at the time of the historic convention.

The Legislative Council of the province of British Columbia, 1871. Amor De Cosmos stands to the right of the steps.

were shaping the new dominion. Despairing of official channels, De Cosmos turned to popular agitation. An ad hoc committee was formed in Victoria, and it sent a memorial directly to Governor General Monck in Ottawa, calling for British Columbia's immediate entry into the dominion, with the sole essential condition that a transcontinental wagon road from the head of Lake Superior to the Pacific should be completed within two years of the colony's admission.

The activities of the Victoria committee had mixed results. One hundred and sixty-four Victorians signed a petition against entry into Confederation, and Helmcken veered to their side. But John Robson, leader of the mainland reformists, finally accepted the confederationist idea and in 1868 supported in the Legislative Council a motion asking for entry into Canada under Clause 146 of the British North America Act, which provided for the eventual inclusion of the colonies of Newfoundland, Prince Edward Island, and British Columbia.

When this motion was defeated by the official members of the council, De Cosmos and his allies formed in May 1868 the Confederation League, the first body resembling a political party ever created in British Columbia. The league's orators toured the colony, and in September 1868 they called together at Yale a "Convention of Delegates, for the purpose of accelerating the admission of the Colony into the Dominion of Canada, upon equitable and beneficial terms, and also to devise means to

Anthony Musgrave, the last governor of British Columbia as a colony, who greatly influenced the progress towards Confederation.

Dr. R. W. W. Carrall arrived in British Columbia to practise as a physician in Barkerville. Later he represented Cariboo in the Legislative Council, and he was one of the delegates whom Governor Musgrave sent to Ottawa in 1970 to discuss the terms of British Columbia's entry into Canada.

In 1870 Joseph W. Trutch, who built part of the Cariboo Road, was British Columbia's commissioner for public works. He also went to Ottawa to discuss confederation terms in 1870, and as a reward for his co-operativeness with the federal authorities he was appointed first lieutenant governor of the new province.

secure Representative Institutions with Responsible Government...."

Twenty-six delegates arrived at Yale from all parts of the province, and their resolutions in favour of Confederation and responsible government won wide support. Yet the official majority in the Legislative Council still opposed Confederation until changing circumstances convinced them that the development was inevitable.

Among these circumstances was the death by dysentery of Governor Seymour in June 1869 while engaged in a minor expedition to quell unrest among the Haida Indians. In his place was appointed Anthony Musgrave, former governor of Newfoundland and a friend of Confederation. It was Musgrave who finally won over the officials so that in April 1870 the Legislative Council at last decided to send a delegation to Ottawa to negotiate British Columbia's entry into the dominion. Having taken the initiative out of the hands of the reformers, the officials proceeded to enjoy their advantage, for when the delegates were chosen, both De Cosmos and Robson were ignored. British Columbia's mandate was borne by Helmcken, Dr. Carrall of the Cariboo, and Joseph Trutch who had helped build the Cariboo Road and, as commissioner of Lands and Works, was an official.

The delegates were welcomed in Ottawa with even better terms than they had asked, for Sir George Etienne Cartier, who led the negotiations in the absence through sickness of Sir John Macdonald, offered not a wagon road but a railway across the prairies to British Columbia, to be commenced in two years and completed in ten. The terms of the agreement were proclaimed on August 30, and a new Legislative Council — now representing the province and no longer the colony of British Columbia — ratified them in January 1871. The colony on the Pacific had become the westernmost rim of a dominion that — as its motto held — stretched from ocean to ocean.

John Sebastian Helmcken had remained active in Pacific Coast politics since the first Vancouver Island Legislative Assembly in 1856. At first doubtful of the value of British Columbia's entering Canada, he later became converted to the idea and was the third member of the delegation to Ottawa in 1870.

J. F. McCreight, the obscure lawyer who became first premier of British Columbia. Eight years after his defeat in 1872 he was appointed a judge of the Supreme Court of British Columbia.

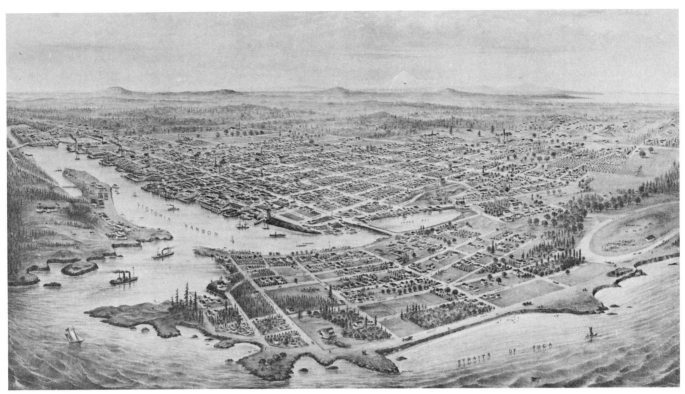

For two decades after Confederation, Victoria remained the leading city of British Columbia. This bird's-eye view, drawn by E. S. Glover in 1878, shows how far it has already spread beyond the tiny area of the original fort.

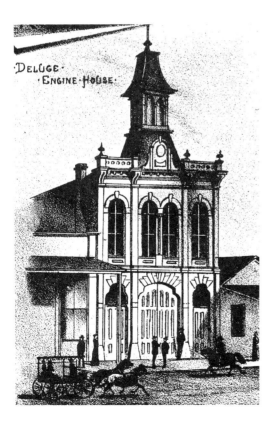

# The Province that Entered Confederation

The British Columbia that entered Confederation was a country almost as large as the original Dominion of Canada, but in its 360,000 square miles hardly more than forty thousand people were living — a shade over one per cent of Canada's total population. And of these forty thousand, almost thirty thousand were native Indians.

The native population had actually been declining for decades and was about a third of what it had been when contact was first made between whites and Indians less than a century before. But the white population was also declining. Even where mining continued, the changed methods and the absence of readily accessible placer gold meant that the masses of fortune hunters who made the great gold rushes of the Fraser and the Cariboo had long departed; the shrinkage of trade which resulted from this exodus had its effect on the coastal communities which depended indirectly on the prosperity of the mining regions.

The population of Victoria, for example, had fallen to four thousand by 1871, and New Westminster could muster not many more than a thousand inhabitants. There were seven hundred people in Nanaimo and the surrounding coal field, and about two thousand remained in Barkerville and scattered through the Cariboo. Between Hope and Boston Bar, in the

The City Hall, which was built in 1873, is still the centre of Victoria's civic life.

Amenities unheard of in early Victoria, like the Royal Hospital (above) and the Deluge Engine House (opposite page, lower left), were changing the city's life.

BRITISH COLUMBIA-THE VICTORIA THEATRE & NEW DRIARD HOTEL.

early mining region of the Fraser Canyon, about a thousand people lived in a number of small communities, of which Yale was the most important, and three or four hundred lived in and around Lillooet. In the vast area north of the Cariboo there were only the Hudson's Bay men in the scattered remaining trading posts, a handful of missionaries, and a few hundred miners working in the Omineca gold field or prospecting over the country and setting off small rushes to creeks that would suddenly be famous and then become the sites of decaying ghost towns. In the Kootenay region also there were a few score men

By the 1880s the Victoria Theatre and the Driard Hotel had moved out of their modest original quarters of gold rush days and combined in a building on Douglas Street where the Hudson's Bay store now stands.

Settlement was spreading outward from Victoria into the rich farmlands of Saanich, and there the pioneers built St. Stephen's Church.

The age of the department store was beginning. Findlay, Durham and Brodie's Victoria House was bought in 1873 by Denny and Spencer. Out of this venture sprang the Spencer chain of department stores which rivalled the Hudson's Bay stores and was eventually taken over by Eatons.

panning gold, but the great mining era of that region, founded on silver and the base metals, had not yet begun.

It was a community slimmed down to a minimum in terms of population, and the period from 1871 to the completion of the Canadian Pacific Railway would see a slow but steady increase in white inhabitants, though the Indian peoples continued to decline until the early years of the present century.

It was also a community finding for itself a much more reliable economic basis than such quickly exhausted resources as fur and gold. The prosperous collieries around Nanaimo were the precursors of a more stable mining industry than that of the colonial decades. Fishing, which had provided the economic base of the prosperous Coast Indian culture, was now being turned to commercial ends by white entrepreneurs who not only caught fish for local consumption but were exporting salted salmon and had already started in a rudimentary way the canning industry that would eventually bring British Columbian salmon to world markets. Farming and cattle raising, which first sprang up to supply the mining settlements, continued now as a stable industry, and in the lower Fraser Valley alone there were about three hundred mixed and dairy farms, while ranching had begun in the grasslands around Ashcroft and Kamloops and at the northern end of the Okanagan Valley.

Perhaps the most important development of the 1860s was the emergence of Burrard Inlet as a harbour whose activities began to rival those of Victoria and New Westminster. The inlet's trade was then based entirely on logging. On the south shore Edward Stamp established Hastings Mill; farther west Jeremiah Rogers ran a spar-cutting operation at Jerry's Cove. On the north shore, at Moodyville, "Sue" Moody had built a steam-driven mill. From both Hastings and Moodyville sailing ships carried sawn lumber and spars to San Francisco and Latin America, to Australia and China, and even to Britain. The mill

Indian fishermen encamped at New Westminster.

Some Victorian houses reflected the dying order of the colonial days, like Sir James Douglas's residence, on whose back verandah Lady Douglas is standing with her brother.

At Fairfield, one of the large new Victorian houses, the gentry rest from the rigours of croquet playing.

Scullers in the 1870s prepare for a race on the Fraser River.

settlements still seemed appendages to New Westminster. Only a few foresightful people had envisaged Burrard Inlet's future as one of Canada's great seaports.

This development of a solid and steady economic foundation for the life of British Columbia meant that the towns of the province, though many of them were little larger than English villages, were already taking on the look of established communities, with regular townsites (usually in the standard North American grid form) and with solid architect-designed buildings beginning to take the place of the more makeshift structures of an earlier era. Many of the buildings that are familiar ornaments of the older British Columbian towns like Victoria date from these early years of British Columbia's existence as a Canadian province.

Early Nanaimo. The Hudson's Bay stockades have vanished but the bastion remained, as it does today.

Already, in trade at least, Burrard Inlet was beginning to threaten the older seaports, as this forest of masts suggests. They belonged to sailing ships loading timber at Hastings Mill where Vancouver now stands.

Across Burrard Inlet at Moodyville, which later became North Vancouver, Moody, Dietz, and Nelson's sawmill figures in an 1872 illustration in the *Canadian Illustrated news.*

In the hinterland, mining was still important, though the emphasis was shifting from gold. H. Perre drew this sketch of a miner's cabin in 1872 at the Eureka Silver Mines.

Local farming had developed, and flour mills like this establishment at Tranquille near Kamloops were appearing in various parts of the province.

# Confederation Imperilled

The Marquis of Dufferin and Ava was Governor General of Canada from 1872 to 1878 and the first incumbent of his office to travel to British Columbia, which he did in 1876.

Lady Dufferin at the time of her visit to British Columbia in 1876.

Among the many sketches Lady Dufferin made on the 1876 viceregal tour was an impression of Indians off the northern coast of the province, paddling out to welcome the Governor General.

The misgivings with which many British Columbians had accepted entry into Canada were sharply increased during the years immediately following Confederation. Secession became a political possibility and remained so throughout the 1870s and even later. It was events in Ottawa rather than in British Columbia that precipitated the situation.

Trouble began when the terms of union were submitted for ratification to the federal parliament in the spring of 1871. Eastern MPs were disturbed by the promise of an expensive railroad across a central plain, inhabited mostly by nomad Indians, and through difficult mountains to reach a province with eleven thousand white inhabitants. Trutch, now lieutenant governor, was in Ottawa for the debates and let Cartier persuade him to concede, during a crucial banquet, that British Columbia "will not regard this railway engagement as a 'cast iron contract', as it has been called, or desire that it should be carried out in any other way than as will secure the prosperity of the whole Dominion of which she is a part."

How Macdonald and Cartier might have taken advantage of this admission is hard to speculate, for in 1873 their government was defeated over scandals in awarding the contract for the Canadian Pacific Railway. But the new Liberal government of Alexander Mackenzie, opposed to rapid construction of a transcontinental railroad, took Trutch at his word.

Meanwhile, in Victoria, the old Legislative Council had been changed for an elected assembly and responsible government. An obscure lawyer, John Foster McCreight, became the province's first premier. By the end of 1872 he was succeeded by Amor De Cosmos, who also held a seat in the federal parliament. Attorney General George Anthony Walkem carried on the actual business of government, while De Cosmos in Ottawa supported Macdonald during the debates on the Pacific Scandal

Lord Dufferin refused to go under this arch in Victoria, which threatened separation unless British Columbia's railway terms were met.

George Anthony Walkem was premier of British Columbia during a large part of the railway crisis, with its threat of secession.

and later tried to salvage what he could of the terms of union from the Mackenzie government. He obtained assurances about a graving dock at Esquimalt, but obviously Mackenzie intended to procrastinate on the issue of the railway, which in British Columbia had not gone beyond the stage of surveys. By 1874 the hostility between the provincial and federal governments had reached the stage where the British government offered to arbitrate. The colonial secretary — Lord Carnarvon — worked out the compromise known as the Carnarvon terms, postponing completion of the transcontinental railway to 1890 but providing for a railway to be built immediately on Vancouver Island between Esquimalt and Nanaimo.

The Senate defeated the Esquimalt and Nanaimo Railway bill, and it became evident that Mackenzie would not keep his bargain. As disillusionment with Canada increased in British Columbia, the Governor General, Lord Dufferin, went there on a pacificatory visit in 1876. His evident concern at the province's mood did not impress Mackenzie. Procrastination endured.

In August 1878 the British Columbian assembly voted to present a memorial to Queen Victoria expressing an intention to withdraw from Confederation in May 1879 unless work had begun on the railway. Shortly afterwards, De Cosmos moved a resolution in the House of Commons that British Columbia should be separated from Canada, though, as he had not arranged for a seconder, he evidently meant this merely as a warning gesture.

But the situation had already changed; the Conservatives had returned to power, committed to Sir John A. Macdonald's National Policy, and though a period of adjustment had to follow before they put their plans into operation, they were clearly committed to completing the transcontinental railway.

The graving dock at Esquimalt, first used by
H.M.S. *Cormorant* in 1887, was British
Columbia's consolation prize for federal delay
in completing the Canadian Pacific Railway.

Surveyors for the Canadian Pacific Railway
working on the Homathco River, inland from
Bute Inlet, before it was finally decided that
the CPR should take the more southerly route
via the Fraser Canyon.

The most distinguished of the surveyors working in British Columbia was G. M. Dawson of the Geological Survey, the smallest of the group, photographed in 1879 at Fort McLeod, the first fur-trading post to be founded by Simon Fraser in British Columbia. Note the legend "Fort Misery" over the doorway, doubtless connected with the swarms of mosquitoes that made Dawson and his companions wear veils tucked up on the brims of their hats.

Surveyors of the 1870s portaging a canoe
between mountain waterways.

Construction in the Fraser Canyon.

# The Railway Completed

Work finally began on the British Columbian section of the Canadian Pacific Railway in May 1880 at Yale, where the American contractor Andrew Onderdonk began blasting a rail bed through the difficult stretches of the Fraser Canyon. There had been considerable discussion and dispute over the route the railway would take. Various ways through the Rockies had been considered before it was finally decided to use the Kicking Horse rather than the Yellowhead Pass.

A number of different tidewater terminals had been suggested. Port Simpson (near the site of Prince Rupert which eventually became the terminus of the Grand Trunk Pacific) was rejected because it might be vulnerable to growing Russian naval strength in the Pacific. Victoria favoured a route that would reach the sea at Bute Inlet, where in 1863-64 Alfred Waddington had tried to build a wagon road, only to have his workers massacred by Chilcotin Indians, an incident which led to the most considerable of British Columbia's very minor Indian wars. From Bute Inlet either a ferry or possibly even an audaciously conceived bridge could carry trains to Vancouver Island, and the Esquimalt and Nanaimo Railway would lead them to a terminus near Victoria. But it was finally the Fraser Valley route, with its terminus at Burrard Inlet, that was chosen, largely to compete with the Northern Pacific Railway being built on American territory to Puget Sound.

If Victoria was disappointed in its hopes of the pride and profit of being a terminus, the mainland went into something of an economic boom; Yale — in long decline after the gold ran out — took on a new life. Workers were needed not only for construc-

William Van Horne, appointed general manager of the Canadian Pacific Railway in 1881, was responsible for the overall construction drive that completed by 1885 the rail link between British Columbia and the rest of Canada.

Work on the coastal section of the railway, including the difficult Fraser Canyon, was under the direction of the American contractor Andrew Onderdonk.

tion but also to work in the improvised factories for making the large quantities of dynamite required for rock clearing. The contractors engaged every available person and then, when there were not enough, began in 1881 to import labourers from China.

William Van Horne, vice-president of the Canadian Pacific Railway in charge of construction, promised that the line would be open to the Pacific by January 1, 1887. In fact, despite recurring financial crises which more than once threatened the existence of the company, the work in the prairies and through the mountains continued with such speed that in August 1885 the new Governor General, Lord Lansdowne, travelled by rail to eighteen miles east of Revelstoke. Forty-seven miles away, on the other side of the gap, he boarded a train that took him to the new settlement of Port Moody, at the head of Burrard Inlet. Three months later, in November, a special train loaded with directors and officials of the Canadian Pacific Railway left Montreal bound for the Pacific. At Eagle Pass in the Monashee Mountains they stopped for the last rail to be laid and for Donald A. Smith, later Lord Strathcona, to drive the legendary last spike. The train then travelled on to the Pacific.

Less than seven months later, on July 4, 1886, the first regular passenger train from Montreal arrived at Port Moody. It was a gala day, but already the fortunes of the little city, where recently land had been selling at speculative prices, were jeopardized by the decision of the Canadian Pacific Railway to extend its line twelve miles along the inlet to Coal Harbour, where Van Horne proposed to establish his final terminus — the future city of Vancouver.

A train of sleighs supplies a CPR construction camp in the Rockies.

Small communities along the CPR route were revitalized by the influx of workers brought by construction. Yale once again became a wild and crowded town, as shown in this sketch drawn in the manner of Pieter Bruegel by an unknown artist.

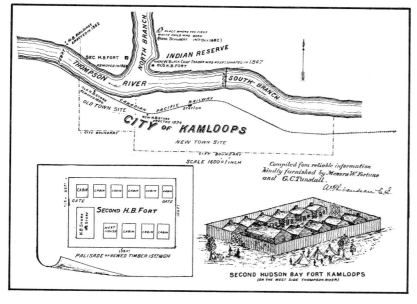

The coming of the railway changed the pattern of settlement. This map of the City of Kamloops in the 1890s shows the Hudson's Bay installations north of the Thompson and the actual city developing south of the river around the railway.

Passengers in a colonist coach of the 1880s on their way to Vancouver.

Surprise Creek Bridge in the Selkirk Mountains was portrayed in the *Illustrated London News*, which closely followed the progress of CPR construction.

On July 4, 1886, the first CPR train reaches
Port Moody.

The end of the line: the first Canadian Pacific
station in Vancouver.

Logging with ox teams on the site of
Vancouver in the early 1880s.

"Gassy Jack" Deighton, who founded the
Deighton Hotel in Gastown during the 1860s.

# The Western Metropolis

The people of Victoria had good reason to be concerned when the terminus of the Canadian Pacific Railway was located on Burrard Inlet, for very soon the new city which sprang up there became the commercial if not the administrative centre of the Pacific Coast and, drawing on the resources of the mainland, outgrew islanded Victoria.

The first white men to settle on the site of Vancouver were three Englishmen — remembered as "the Three Greenhorns" — who heard of the discovery of coal there and staked a claim on the land between Coal Harbour and English Bay. They made bricks — the first on the mainland — rather than digging coal.

In the 1860s the resort known as the Brighton Hotel was built on a place which in 1869 was named Hastings after Rear-Admiral George Fowler Hastings, commander of the Royal Navy's Pacific station. And here, close to Edward Stamp's Hastings Mill, the retired river pilot "Gassy Jack" Deighton built the Deighton Hotel, a less elegant establishment than the Brighton; it was patronized by millhands and seamen. The little settlement that sprang up under Gassy Jack's loquacious patronage was called Gastown (a name it has since recovered), but in 1870 its inhabitants renamed it Granville in honour of the incumbent colonial secretary in Westminster.

During the 1880s development moved westward. A new community, to be called the City of Liverpool, was laid out by speculators between Coal Harbour and the present site of Georgia Street, but nothing came of it. Only in 1885, when the CPR surveyor L. A. Hamilton laid out a townsite where Van Horne had selected the spot for his terminus, was the street plan of downtown Vancouver established. It was Van Horne, perhaps seeking a partial echo of his own name, who insisted that the place be named Vancouver, and such it became — to the rage of Vancouver Islanders — when the city was incorporated on April 6, 1886.

An early act of the newly elected city council was to petition the federal government to allot them the area of wild land known as Coal Peninsula which had been set aside as a military reserve for fortifications protecting the harbour. The area was granted to the city in perpetual lease. Two years later, in September 1888, one of the finest of the world's parks was opened there by Lord Stanley, after whom it was named.

On land that was being logged off by the Oppenheimer brothers and the Three Greenhorns, a makeshift town rose quickly in the spring of 1886; by the time fire swept through and destroyed it in June 1886, there were eight hundred buildings, most of which housed businesses, and two thousand inhabitants. The city rose again like a phoenix from the fire; at the end of 1887 there were five thousand people there, and by 1889, with

Vancouver four weeks after the great fire of June 1886. The line of forest runs across what is now Burrard Street. The smoke is from land-clearing fires where Richards, Granville, and Hornby streets now run in the heart of modern Vancouver.

David Oppenheimer, the first mayor of Vancouver.

eight thousand inhabitants, Vancouver was beginning to outgrow Victoria.

Not only was it the terminus of the CPR, into which the first passenger train ran on May 23, 1887. Its future as a great seaport began to take shape when the liner *Abyssinia*, chartered from the Cunard Line, arrived from China on June 14. Four years later, in 1891, the *Empress of Japan*, first of the CPR's own elegant Orient liners, sailed into the harbour with Her Majesty's mail from Hong Kong to Britain.

By now Vancouver was a town with factories and foundries, with thirty-six miles of streets and a tramway linking it to New Westminster, with a great brick railway hotel — the first Hotel Vancouver — and an opera house.

At the end of the railroad that united three thousand miles of territory, Vancouver, more than any other city, absorbed the westward flow of population, investment, and enterprise that came with the completion of the transcontinental railroad, and by the beginning of the 1890s it was already well on its way to becoming the metropolis of western Canada.

Early Granville Street at the end of 1886, seen from the newly built Hotel Vancouver.

A waterfront view of Vancouver from the CPR docks in the summer of 1887.

As Vancouver grew rapidly from a shacktown to a city, Moodyville on the north shore of Burrard Inlet continued to prosper. R.Maynard, one of the best photographers of the time, took this picture of sailing ships loading there in 1888.

103

Among the many establishments created
during the early years of Vancouver was its
first Hudson's Bay store, opened in January
1887.

Only a few years afterwards, trade had
outgrown the original Hudson's Bay store and
a new four-storey red-brick building was
constructed at the corner of Georgia and
Granville streets. It was opened in 1893. The
streetcar tracks were laid in 1890, three years
after Vancouver's incorporation.

# Recognizing the Landscape

Politically, the completion of the Canadian Pacific Railway consolidated the imperilled unity of British Columbia with the rest of Canada. Economically, it provided the artery through which the province's resources could flow out to the rest of the country and through which population could flow in. But there were less material ways in which the coming of the railroad affected life west of the Rockies; one of them lay in the artistic awakening of the region and the foundation of a western tradition of landscape painting.

It was not until the turn of the century that notable native painters began to emerge in British Columbia, such as Emily Carr and Sophie Pemberton. Up to that time the painters who visually interpreted the province came mainly from England and eastern Canada, using whatever transport offered itself. Paul Kane travelled by the fur traders' canoe routes; William G. R. Hind accompanied the overlanders; Frederick Whymper followed the goldminers north from San Francisco; and as late as 1882 the Canadian landscapist Lucius O'Brien travelled by horseback from Chicago to the Canadian Rockies and thence to the Pacific Coast.

But it was with the completion of the Canadian Pacific Railway that the artistic exploration of British Columbia began in real earnest. By penetrating through the great passes of the

*Boat Encampment* by Paul Kane.

*Fort Yale, B.C.* by Frederick Whymper.

*A British Columbian Forest* by Lucius R. O'Brien.

*The Rogers Pass* by John Arthur Fraser.

Rockies, the Selkirks, and the Monashees, the railway made the magnificent mountain scenery of the province far more accessible than at any time in the past. And the railway officials lavishly encouraged every painter of talent who wished to accept the artistic challenges the landscape offered.

It was mainly William Van Horne who inspired this policy. This ruthless and highly capable organizer was also himself a skilful amateur painter and one of the most discerning art collectors of his era. He realized what the Canadian Pacific's route had to offer the painters of his time, who were still devoted to the representation and interpretation of the world of nature. But he also understood the kind of publicity which paintings of the railway's terrain by well-known artists could bring, not only in Canada but also abroad. Therefore he was very free with his passes, and the artists gladly accepted them.

Many painters came for several years running. Artists like Lucius O'Brien, J. A. Fraser, Edward Roper, F. M. Bell-Smith, Thomas Mower Martin, and even that talented amateur, Queen Victoria's son-in-law the Marquis of Lorne, not only recorded their impressions of the high mountains but also discovered the varying charms of the dry lands and the lush valleys, the coastal rain forests and the endlessly complicated inlets and islands.

The Marquis of Lorne, Governor General of
Canada from 1878 to 1883, was not only a
zealous patron of the arts, founder of the
National Gallery of Canada and the Royal
Canadian Academy but he was also an
enthusiastic amateur artist. Frederick
Whymper included an engraving of Lorne's
drawing entitled *Road Near New
Westminster, British Columbia: Douglas Fir
and Gigantic Cedar* in his *Canadian Pictures*
(c. 1884).

The Marquis of Lorne and his wife Princess
Louise, who was Queen Victoria's daughter.

Some of them, especially Mower Martin, revived Paul Kane's interest in the Indian peoples whose culture in the 1880s was reaching its last flowering, and their paintings of native people still living a traditional life formed a link with the splendid and sombre works in which, early in the new century, Emily Carr began to record with elegiac power the monuments that survived of a culture which already seemed dead, or at least moribund.

*Mount Field and Mount Stephen* by Edward Roper.

*Westcoast Indians Returning from the Hunt* by Thomas Mower Martin.

*Blunden Harbour* by Emily Carr.

# Confederation and the Indians

When British Columbia entered Confederation, three-quarters of its inhabitants were Indians. They were not citizens of the colony and they did not become citizens of the dominion. Moreover, there was never a treaty between Canada and the Indians of the province as a whole, similar to those concluded with native peoples east of the Rockies.

During the colonial period there had been a variety of policies towards the Indians. The fur traders left them virtually alone unless they endangered European lives, when they were quickly dealt with — as when in 1853 Douglas got together a volunteer company, the Victoria Voltigeurs, to hunt down a murderer among the Cowichan band on Vancouver Island. Later, when the miners arrived, there was sporadic fighting over trespass on hunting lands, but until the 1860s no serious attempt was made to interfere in the wars between the Indians themselves, intensified by the availability of firearms freely sold by the traders. It was only at times like the Chilcotin war of 1863-64, when white men had been massacred, or on the increasingly rare occasions when coastal boats were attacked that the Royal Navy was called in or that militia forces campaigned against the native warriors — always, by dint of superior arms, successfully.

As fur-trading and mining gave way to settlement, Indian lands became a crucial question, for traditional fishing and hunting rights extended over great areas that white men wished to exploit. Under colonial administrations, treaties were made with some bands, but in many cases land was arbitrarily pre-empted for logging or erecting canneries. After Confederation, the Indians themselves became theoretically wards of the dominion, but jurisdiction over lands was provincial and disputes between the two levels of government extended into the 1920s. They ended with the Indians being allotted as reserves some

John Webber's *Woman of Nootka Sound* shows an Indian of the British Columbian Coast at the time of first contact when Cook landed on Vancouver Island in 1778.

Paul Kane's *Babbine Chief* portrays one of the many Indians who came down from the north shortly after the foundation of Fort Victoria. By the 1840s they were deeply involved in the trading complex established by the Europeans, though already there had been other forms of acculturation between native peoples — this chief of an inland Carrier tribe wears a Chilkat blanket made by the coastal Tlingit and a painted hat in the Haida pattern.

As the gold miners pressed up the Fraser Canyon in 1858-59, they came upon the burying grounds of the Salish Indians. Frederick Whymper painted such a beflagged cemetery near Boston Bar.

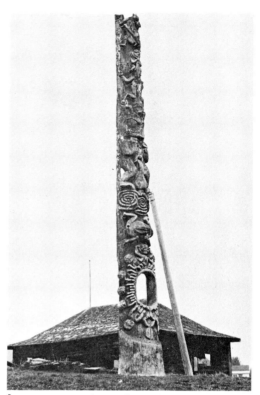

In some parts, the traditional arts of the Coast were continued until relatively late, especially on the geographically isolated Upper Skeena. The famous Hole-in-the-Sky pole at Kitwancool may have been carved round about 1880; other poles in the region were carved as late as the early 1920s and raised at illegal potlatches.

The villages of the Haida with their groves of carved poles excited the imagination of travelling artists like Rudolph Cronau, who painted this rather Wagnerian water colour in the early 1880s.

843,000 acres — round about 1,300 square miles — less than 0.4 per cent of the province over which they had freely hunted. To this day, the Indians have disputed this injustice, and their claims to large areas of the province are still active.

In other respects the results of Indian-white contact were complex. White men's diseases — smallpox and influenza, measles and syphilis — reduced the Indian population by the early twentieth century to a mere twenty-two thousand, a quarter the aboriginal population when Cook landed. Yet, paradoxically, the Indian culture was in many ways stimulated by contact. The marine fur traders, greedy for otter skins, brought large quantities of iron tools, and a minor technological revolution took place. Now the Indians could carve far more quickly than with stone and jade tools, and the quantity of poles, masks, and ceremonial objects increased phenomenally, while ease of production allowed a new fluency of style. Almost all the great artifacts now representing the Coast Indian culture in world museums date from between the early nineteenth century and its final decades when the culture fell into decay.

The increased production of artifacts gained most meaning in Indian terms because the enormous simultaneous increase in merchandise earned by trading and working for white employers enabled the Coast peoples to indulge in more numerous and lavish potlatches, the giving feasts where titles were validated and masked dances displayed. At the same time, the dramatic winter dances of the Kwakiutl increased in complexity and provided further means by which the Indians could indulge their desire to display and enhance the names and ranks they owned.

Here a tragic factor intervened. The reduction of population meant there were fewer people to compete for the ancient titles, which were only valid if they had been witnessed at potlatches. As the leading nobles died, distantly related commoners struggled to assume their titles, and the potlatches became competitions in the display and often the destruction of wealth.

To many missionaries and federal Indian agents, brought up with Calvinist ideas of prudence and thrift, the whole concept of

Having their own ceremonial finery, Coast Indians were fascinated by the formal garb of other cultures, and often, like these Haida chiefs, they would appear in the dress of European military glory or civilian respectability without seeing any incongruity with their traditions.

the potlatch was alarming. They persuaded Sir John A. Macdonald, who retained control of Indian affairs even when he was prime minister, to pass in 1884 a regulation forbidding both the potlatch and the Salish spirit dances. It was a direct attack on central institutions in the Coast Indian culture.

At first, the law was disallowed by Judge Begbie, who knew more about the realities of Indian life than the officials in Ottawa did, but it was revised and reinstated. There followed a kind of guerrilla campaign between Indians and agents, the former carrying on their potlatches secretly, the latter prosecuting where they could, until the famous and gigantic potlatch of Dan Cranmer on Village Island in 1921, when thirty chiefs were prosecuted and only those who gave up their potlatch regalia to the RCMP were set free. Only in 1951 was the potlatch law repealed and the Indians allowed to enjoy their ceremonials without interference.

By that time the traditional economic base of Indian life had been destroyed, the old communal houses had been replaced by Canadian villas, the arts had become stagnant, and even the people who attempted to revive their ancient rituals lived everyday lives like other Canadians. A few, by fishing or land deals, were prosperous; most were poor.

E. S. Curtis reached the Coast when the culture was already in retreat, but he persuaded Indians who still possessed their regalia to stage spectacles reminiscent of their past; among his more dramatic photographs was this assemblage of Kwakiutl masked dancers, taken at the turn of the century.

Another kind of acculturation was the use of European materials, like woollen blankets, to make ceremonial garments whose designs were entirely within the Indian traditions.

The absorption of western techniques and products into the Coast Indian culture was nowhere more strikingly demonstrated than in the potlatches, where large quantities of manufactured goods were given away according to ancient and strictly maintained traditional protocol.

# Duncan of Metlakatla
## and the Anglican Schism

Missionaries of all kinds, from Catholics and Anglicans to Methodists and Salvationists, played a great part in the acculturation of the Indians of the Pacific Coast. The conversions were finally almost complete. Some of the local Indians evolved sects of their own that combined Christian concepts with the remnants of aboriginal beliefs — like the Shaker Church, with its holy dancing and deafening handbell ringing, which became popular among the Salish — but most of the native peoples now belong to regular churches and are a good deal more pious than most of their white neighbours even when, as among the Kwakiutl and the Gitksan, they have been active in reviving ancient ceremonials. They have recognized that the old and the new moralities are not irreconcilable.

The most famous missionary of British Columbia was William Duncan, whose reputation rests partly on the role he played in a lasting schism within the Church of England in British Columbia. Duncan, a former leather merchant, arrived in

Salvationist converts on the Skeena River.

Victoria in 1857 as a lay missionary, which he remained to the end of his stormy life, never taking Anglican orders. He immediately made friends with Edward Cridge, the aggressively Low-Church Hudson's Bay chaplain who had arrived in 1854. Duncan also had the support of Captain Prevost, a senior naval commander, and this helped him overcome James Douglas's objections (in Douglas's role as Hudson's Bay chief factor) to his starting a mission among the turbulent Tsimshian who had settled around the trading post of Fort Simpson.

Duncan went north almost immediately, carefully learnt the Tsimshian tongue and then, not without risk, set about preaching in the great communal houses of the village. Some of the chiefs supported him, but Duncan quickly saw that this was a matter of rivalry in terms of prestige and that the pagan way of life, with its shamanism and its ritual cannibal ceremonies, was little changed. He decided to make a clean break by withdrawing the converted.

In 1862 he established a model mission village in the protected channel of Metlakatla. He withdrew his followers just in time, for shortly afterwards smallpox swept through Fort Simpson; Metlakatla was untouched, and Duncan's prestige soared. He

William Duncan at the height of his missionary enterprise.

Haida women in the Queen Charlottes, weaving baskets in the 1880s.

117

Metlakatla and its great church were visited by the Governor General, Lord Dufferin, in 1876, and Lady Dufferin drew this sketch of Duncan's model village.

created a neat replica of an English village, with an enormous wooden Gothic church, industries, a local police force, and small family houses. But he displeased the Anglican authorities by refusing to allow Holy Communion to be administered even when ordained priests arrived, since he rightly feared that the Indians would find it hard to distinguish between the symbolic eating of Christ's body in the form of bread and their own ritual cannibalism during the Hamatsa ceremony.

Duncan's disputes with the Church Missionary Society and with George Hills — ordained bishop of Columbia in 1860 — were encouraged by his friend Cridge, who had become dean of Christ Church Cathedral in Victoria and was carrying on a running feud with the tractarian Hills over High-Church rituals. The Cridge-Hills dispute split the ranks of Victorian Anglicanism, and when Cridge resigned to join the Reformed Episcopal Church in 1874, Sir James Douglas and many others of his congregation joined his new Church of Our Lord. Cridge became a bishop of the Reformed Episcopal Church in 1875.

Cridge had supported Duncan in his disputes, and the formidable founder of Metlakatla found it easy to maintain the autonomy of his fief against the efforts of the distant Bishop Hills in Victoria. But his opposition to the administration of the sacrament of Holy Communion seemed increasingly heretical to the Church Missionary Society, and in 1879, when a new diocese of New Caledonia was created, Bishop William Ridley was allowed to set up his headquarters in the heart of Duncan's domain, at Metlakatla.

Several years of ecclesiastical feuding ensued. Ridley won only a few of the Indians to his side, but he recruited the support of the provincial government. At last, impatient with state as well as church bureaucracy, Duncan departed for Annette Island in Alaskan waters, taking the majority of his Tsimshian followers with him, to found a second successfully self-supporting missionary village, New Metlakatla. Duncan's Indian converts never returned to Canada, and the schism which was started by Cridge's secession continues even today; the Reformed Episcopal movement did not re-enter the Anglican fold, and its churches still flourish in Victoria, New Westminster, and other British Columbian cities.

Dean Edward Cridge in his old age as Bishop Cridge of the Reformed Episcopal Church.

When Edward Cridge departed from the Church of England, his many sympathizers built for him in Victoria, between 1874 and 1876, the Church of Our Lord.

When Sir James Douglas died, the most impressive funeral yet held in Victoria took place — not at Bishop Hill's Christ Church Cathedral up on the hill but at his friend Cridge's Church of Our Lord.

Crowded Chinese dwellings in Victoria during the 1880s helped to foster anti-Oriental feeling.

## Facing the Yellow Peril!

Perhaps the first Asians to reach British Columbia crossed the Bering Strait in the distant millennia at the end of the Ice Age and became the ancestors of our native Indians. But in terms of known history, they were the Chinese who — like the first British Columbian blacks — arrived with the gold miners from California in 1858. There were enough of them to establish the nucleus of a Chinatown in Victoria and to form small exotic enclaves in the mining settlements. They provided services as laundrymen; they panned the less profitable bars or the tailings that other miners had abandoned; and as the placer mining era receded, they worked as labourers for the mining syndicates — which brought them into competition with white men needing work, who found that the Chinese would accept lower wages. Anti-Chinese feeling began to emerge in the early 1860s, and it increased as the province moved into economic recession towards the end of the decade.

During the 1870s a second wave of Chinese began to arrive, brought directly from Kwang Tung by labour contractors. They worked on farms, in the new fish canneries, and as domestic servants. By 1880 there were four thousand Chinese in the

Two typical Chinese labourers working on CPR construction. Many died from fever in the mountain terrain of British Columbia.

province, against twenty thousand Caucasians; and the nascent labour unions, particularly the Knights of Labour, were militantly opposed to importing more of them. In 1878 the British Columbian legislature banned their employment in public works, and in 1879 Amor De Cosmos supported in the dominion parliament a petition by fifteen hundred British Columbian working men asking for an end to Chinese immigration; in 1880 he presented another.

By this time, however, with the decision to resume work on the Canadian Pacific, it was evident that there was not enough white labour. Andrew Onderdonk, contractor for the most difficult sections of the railway, had the support of Sir John A. Macdonald when he began to import Chinese by the shipload from Hong Kong. Admitting that he did not believe the Chinese could "assimilate with our Arian population," Sir John declared in the House of Commons in 1882, "Either you have this labour or you can't have the railway." In that year Onderdonk imported six thousand Chinese labourers. They worked for a dollar a day and were far more willing than the white workers to be moved quickly from job to job. They accepted dangerous tasks, and to this day we only know that many Chinese died in the building of the CPR; we do not know how many.

Altogether, between 1881 and 1884, more than ten thousand

Amor De Cosmos gained local support for his demand in 1879 for an end to Chinese immigration, but critics in other parts of Canada, like the cartoonist for the *Canadian Illustrated News*, found inconsistency between De Cosmos's anti-Orientalism and the universal love implied in his assumed name.

The Joss-house, or Chinese temple, in Victoria was one of the more exotic sights of the city in the 1880s.

Chinese arrived in British Columbian ports and another four thousand via American ports. They brought no women, since they intended to return home when they had earned enough money. Many did, but enough remained after railway construction came to an end to provide competition for white workers, who became bitter opponents of Asian immigration, particularly after 1883 when Robert Dunsmuir used Chinese labourers to break a strike in his Vancouver Island mines. In 1887, in Vancouver, the first anti-Chinese riots took place.

The provincial government attempted to impose regulations based on those in Natal, which made language proficiency a test for entry. These were disallowed by the federal government, and instead, a series of head taxes were imposed, beginning at $50 in 1885, rising to $100 in 1901 (by which time there were almost fourteen thousand Chinese in the province), and rising to $500 in 1905. These measures temporarily discouraged the flow and they were reinforced by restrictive regulations that culminated in 1923 in the Chinese Immigration Act, which kept out everyone except diplomatic personnel. Not until the 1960s would the restrictions be entirely lifted and the Chinese allowed equal status with other peoples as immigrants.

The Japanese did not begin to arrive until the 1890s, but during that decade they began to play an increasing role in the fishing industry, which was part of the reason for the fishermen's

Mrs. R. P. Rithet's houseboy in Victoria. Many Chinese worked as domestic servants in the larger houses of Victoria and Vancouver, and gave the West Coast merchant class a way of life in some ways resembling that of their counterparts of the China coast.

strike of 1900 and for the serious Vancouver riots against both Chinese and Japanese in 1907. Instead of legislation, diplomatic negotiations with the Japanese government were used to relieve this situation, with the result that after 1908 the flow of Japanese immigrants was considerably reduced. Japanese — both immigrants and native born — became the target of special discrimination after Pearl Harbour. On February 26, 1942, some 23,000 people of Japanese origin were expelled from the British Columbian coast to places in the interior of the province and even to other parts of Canada. Non-portable property, like farms or fishing boats, was confiscated. No charge of disloyalty was ever in fact proved against any person of Japanese descent in Canada, and the incident has long been regarded in British Columbia as a cause for shame.

To counter prejudice, the Chinese were demonstrative in their loyalty to the British crown and were among the first to raise welcoming arches for visiting dignitaries, like this one erected by the Chinese community of Nanaimo.

In spite of persecution and the virtual end of
immigration, communities like the now-
demolished Chinatown of Duncan continued
to exist even in the lesser towns of the
province.

Vancouver's Chinatown in the early 1960s.
The effects of liberalized immigration policies
had not yet been felt, and aging males still
tended to dominate the Chinese population.

The hospital for Japanese fishermen at Steveston. Founded in the 1890s (the group photograph was taken in 1897), this establishment continued until the expulsion of the Japanese from the Coast in 1942.

# The Rush to the Kootenays

The Kootenays and the boundary region in British Columbia form a triangle of mountains and narrow valleys between Okanagan Lake and the Rocky Mountains. Gold was found at Rock Creek in 1860 and shortly afterwards at Big Bend on the Columbia River, and small rushes continued in the area over the next twenty years without the prospectors recognizing the real wealth that lay in the region.

It was in the 1880s that the first important discoveries began, with the opening of the Blue Bell silver-lead mine near Nelson in 1882, followed by similar discoveries in the Slocan area and the finding of copper at Phoenix. Early in the 1890s the Le Roi and other mines on Red Mountain were discovered and the unruly town of Rossland sprang up. Other celebrated mines were discovered shortly afterwards, like the Sullivan at Kimberley (which still — eighty years afterwards — produces ore in abundance), the Slocan Star in the Slocan Valley, and the Nickel Plate in the Similkameen Valley. And in 1895, when the price of silver rose on

The Ibex Mine in the Slocan district, seen from the upper workings.

One of the many mountain railways built in the 1890s ran between Kaslo on Kootenay Lake and Slocan Lake. This view at Payne Bluff is typical of the kind of construction work involved.

Sandon, established in 1892, the year after Jack Sandon found mineral ore in the area, was situated in a valley of the Selkirks. Like so many of the mining centres of the period, it is now a ghost town so ravaged by fires and floods and winter storms that very little remains standing.

world markets, the rush to the Kootenays and the boundary region was on.

Again, as in the Fraser Valley rush, it was dominated by Americans. But this time there were considerable differences. In the Kootenays no overnight fortunes waited to be made by individuals as in the placer mining era. A few prospectors might make lucky finds, but these could only be exploited by combines with the capital needed for large-scale mining operations. Consequently, most of the population of the new and boisterous towns that sprang up (and often wasted away in a decade or so into ghost towns — like Rossland and Nelson, Slocan City and Sandon, and later Grand Forks and Greenwood) were wage earners, who brought with them the militant unionism of such labour organizations as the Industrial Workers of the World (the famous Wobblies) and the Western Federation of Miners.

The new style of mining led to a partial industrialization of the region. At first, the ore from the Kootenay mines was taken down for smelting to the United States, but in 1895 F. Augustus Heinze established the smelter at Trail, and shortly afterwards others were built at Grand Forks and Greenwood.

The appearance of the smelters coincided with the second wave of British Columbia railway building. By the 1880s the Dewdney Trail over the mountains from Hope to Similkameen

The miners of Sandon hold a rock-drilling contest in 1904. McDonald and McGilvery are the men stripped for action.

By 1914 the slag piles of the Granby smelter at Grand Forks had grown to vast black pyramids, which still dominate the valley long after the smelter has shut down.

and farther east had fallen out of use and become impassable. When the Canadian Pacific Railway was completed, wagon trails were made southward from Revelstoke and Golden to link up with the West and East Kootenays respectively, but transport by such routes was expensive, and it was obvious that whoever could provide an effective railway link would be able to profit from the boom in this southwestern corner of the province.

American railway interests operating out of Spokane and Tacoma were anxious to divert the trade of this rich region into their own systems, but in the end it was the Canadian Pacific

The largest of the smelters, which has survived all the rest, was that operated by Cominco in Trail, here photographed in the early 1900s.

Railway that emerged victorious, acquiring Heinze's railroad charters, together with his smelter (which eventually became the nucleus of Cominco). In 1897 the CPR built a line from Lethbridge through the recently opened Crowsnest Pass coalfield to Kootenay Lake, from which branch lines probed into the Slocan and other mining regions. As in the Cariboo, the farmers followed the miners to provide for their needs, and with the development of agriculture and ranching, the whole southwestern region began to play a leading role in the economy of British Columbia and, inevitably, in its changing political life.

Rossland, founded by Ross Thompson in
1892, was probably the wildest and most
colourful of the Kootenay mining cities. The
Strand, photographed about 1900, was one of
its many saloons.

# The Politics of Plunder

From British Columbia's entry into Canada in 1871 down to the completion of the CPR in 1885, politics on the Pacific Coast had been dominated by the overriding question of the railway, which the people of the region recognized was the clue to the unlocking of the vast resources their province had to offer. Even during that period, the allocation of those resources had acquired growing importance, particularly as the men who were elected to the legislature, and as MPs to the dominion parliament, were often themselves either property owners or deeply involved in the province's rising primary industries.

Amor De Cosmos had speculated in land since the late 1850s, first at Fort Langley and New Westminster, and then in Victoria, while in the 1870s he and another provincial premier, George Walkem, were involved and barely exonerated in a scandal over land deals on Texada Island. Their accuser at the time was John Robson, but Robson himself had acquired enough land on the site of Vancouver by the time the Canadian Pacific reached there to make him a rich man. Robert Dunsmuir, the Nanaimo coal magnate who made an immense fortune out of the mines at Wellington on Vancouver Island, also entered provincial politics, was elected to the Legislative Assembly in 1882 and in 1886 became president of the council; his son James became premier of the province in 1900.

The advent of the railway gave an impetus to every kind of exploitation of natural resources. Fishing ceased to be mainly a

A symbol of the expansive new politics of late nineteenth-century British Columbia was the new Parliament Building, completed in 1897. It was designed by the English architect Francis Mawson Rattenbury, who helped change the face of turn-of-the-century Victoria before he was murdered by his wife's lover — who was also his chauffeur. This unique photograph was taken immediately after completion, when the old government buildings (the Birdcages) were still standing in the foreground.

Robert Dunsmuir, son of a Scottish coal master, came to Vancouver Island in 1850 and worked as a mining expert at Nanaimo until he discovered a rich vein of coal at nearby Wellington, on which he built a fortune that led him into railway speculation and politics.

The Vancouver Coal Mining Company's mine at Nanaimo, where Dunsmuir worked before he developed his own mines.

subsistence occupation of Indians and was dominated by the canneries that appeared on every channel and estuary where the salmon migrated from the sea to the spawning grounds. Ranching emerged as a major industry, largely encouraged by the fact that up to 1884 land could be pre-empted at a dollar an acre and grazing land could be leased at an annual rent of no more than six cents an acre. Many of the great British Columbian ranches were established during this period in the Cariboo and Nicola regions.

Timber had already begun to boom in the late 1860s when the great mills were built on Burrard Inlet, and during the next two decades successive provincial governments did everything they could to encourage the timber magnates with advantageous terms. "Until 1888," said Margaret Ormsby in *British Columbia: A History* (1958), "timber leases could be acquired at an annual rental ranging from one to ten cents an acre and the payment of a royalty of 20 to 25 cents per thousand feet. At the rate of one cent an acre, the owners of the Moody Sawmill, who included Hugh Nelson, now Lieutenant-Governor of the province, leased 17 square miles of coastal timber at the head of Burrard Inlet; the Hastings Sawmill, some 18,500 acres in the same vicinity; and R. P. Rithet, 15,000 acres on Vancouver Island."

Nor were the railways backward in acquiring benefits. The Canadian Pacific's substantial land grants included 6,000 acres in the heart of Vancouver, whose manipulation still, in 1980, contributes substantially to the company's prosperity. By buying up various small railways in the Kootenays during the 1890s, the CPR acquired another 750,000 acres in that region.

Provincial politics during this period were afflicted by a high mortality among premiers. William Smithe, who had become premier in 1883 and welcomed the first CPR train in 1886, died in 1887. His successor, A. E. B. Davie, lived long enough to change the timber rights legislation so that rentals were raised to five cents an acre and royalties to fifty cents a thousand feet, and then died in July 1889. The shifting pattern of factions which in

VANCOUVER COAL MINING CO'S SHAFT No. 1.
NANAIMO B.C.

Dunsmuir is said to have promised his wife a castle if she went with him to British Columbia. Eventually, he built it in Victoria, of solid granite cut by masons brought from Scotland. It cost $650,000 and he called it Craigdarroch, but he never lived in it, for he died a few months before it was finished. The "castle", proving unsalable, was finally disposed of in a dollar raffle.

R. P. Rithet was another of the great speculators in late-Victorian British Columbia. A wealthy wholesale merchant, Rithet later became involved in land and lumber speculation, and was granted fifteen thousand acres of timber on Vancouver Island at a rent of one cent an acre.

The activities of land speculators in British Columbia and their links with local politicians aroused the interest of the formidable Toronto caricaturist J. W. Bengough. In 1890, in his cartoon *Light Breaking in the Far West* (above), he showed approval of Premier Robson's attempts to end the fleecing of the public by land speculators. But by 1892 renewed land grabs by the railways led him — in *Van's Reserve Pudding* (above right) — to portray "the Napoleonic Van Horne" with the provincial government in his pocket.

the absence of provincial political parties still dominated the legislature, now threw up John Robson, the radical of the 1860s who had become a rich landowner. By this time criticism of the government giveaways to the great vested interests had become so loud that Robson had to initiate the first effective legislation relating to resources when in 1892 he amended the Land and Mineral acts: mineral and water resources were vested in the crown, mineral resources were excepted from railway land grants, limits were placed on the sale of timber lands, and no more than a square mile of surveyed crown lands could be sold to any one individual. Having completed this task, Robson succumbed to the fate of his predecessors, dying later in 1892 from blood poisoning through squeezing his finger in the door of a London cab.

His successor, Theodore Davie, presided over the construction of a splendid new parliament building which still houses the government of British Columbia; but this seemed for long an ironic symbol of prosperity, since by the time it was completed the Vancouver boom had collapsed, the great flood of 1894 had devastated the farmlands of the Fraser Valley, and the only people to profit by the depression were large companies who bought up failing ventures in the canning and timber industries. The growing activity in the metal mines of the Kootenays helped mitigate the economic crisis, but it was not until the Klondike gold rush of 1898 created an atmosphere in the larger cities similar to that of the 1858 Fraser Valley rush that Vancouver and Victoria began to climb back to prosperity.

The Coldstream Ranch near Vernon, one of the early farms of the Okanagan, painted by John Hammond in 1896.

Fortune hunters at the Victoria Customs House on Wharf Street in 1898, seeking licences for the Klondike.

Klondikers with their outfits ready for shipment outside E. J. Saunders & Co., the leading miners' outfitters in Victoria, in April 1898.

# Highways by Land and Water

The completion of the Canadian Pacific Railway left the transportation patterns of large areas of British Columbia virtually unchanged. Places along the line of the railway, like Golden and Revelstoke and Kamloops, became trans-shipment centres for goods brought in on wagon roads and so opened up some of the adjacent areas. In 1886 the Esquimalt and Nanaimo Railway had been completed on Vancouver Island. But not until the late 1890s did railway construction reach the Kootenays, and only on the eve of World War I did the Grand Trunk Pacific and the Canadian Northern take their tracks into the northern part of the province. Barkerville, the heart of the Cariboo, was never reached by rail.

The wagon roads with their horse transport remained important throughout the century, and outlying regions where roads gave way to trails were served by pack trains of mules and horses, though more exotic forms of transport (like the ox trains of the early days and the camels that Frank Laumeister used briefly on the Cariboo Road in the 1860s) quickly fell out of use.

High traffic on the Cariboo Road: ox wagons passing through Boston Bar in the early 1880s.

After the CPR was completed, non-mechanical transport still prevailed north of the tracks. A six-horse team arrives at Cottonwood House, the halfway inn on the road to Barkerville.

On the coast, steam navigation by side-wheelers had existed ever since the *Beaver* arrived in the 1830s, and by the 1880s screw steamers were plying up the inlets and between the off-shore islands. Stern-wheelers had operated on the lower Fraser as far as Yale since the gold rush of 1858, and shortly afterwards on the upper Fraser above the canyon. After the completion of the Canadian Pacific, the various great lakes of the province became important links in the transportation system; regular steamboat services were established on Okanagan, Kootenay, Slocan, and the Arrow lakes, and early in the twentieth century, on northern rivers — the Skeena and the Nass.

The difficulty of transport in a mountainous country like British Columbia and the length of necessary journeys led to an early interest in mechanical forms of transport. Proposals for using steam on the Cariboo Road were being made not long after it was completed, and horseless carriages appeared in Vancouver before the end of the 1890s. Automobiles were in use all over the province, at least in small numbers, by the end of the Edwardian era; novelty and fashion in this area reinforced necessity.

This was also the era of the bicycle vogue and, at the other extreme, of the first aeroplanes, which began to fly in British Columbian air during the early years of the century, mainly operated by amateurs. But it was not until after World War I that the Rockies were crossed by air and the first bush pilots laid the foundations of the later commercial airlines.

Horse stages operated in many parts until World War I. The last mail coach that ran from Victoria to Colwood and Metchosin was still preserved in the 1960s.

Once Vancouver had arisen as terminal city of the CPR it became the centre of coastal feeder routes operated by ships like the *Islander* of the Canadian Steam Navigation Company.

The lakes of British Columbia also became highways. In this water colour, Cleveland Rockwell shows a steam launch operating on Harrison Lake in 1895.

Building a stern-wheeler at Fort Alexandria on the Fraser River.

The *Inlander* stern-wheeler on the Skeena River, steaming in 1911 into the difficult waters of Kitselas Canyon.

Long before locomotive whistles echoed in the Rockies, steam transport was in the minds of British Columbians, as this 1871 advertisement in the *British Colonist* shows.

STEAM TO CARIBOO !

*The British Columbia*
GENERAL TRANSPORTATION COMPANY

Will place Four of THOMSON'S PATENT ROAD STEAM-ERS on the route between Yale and Barkerville in the First Week in April, and will be prepared to enter into Contracts for the conveyance of Freight from Yale to Soda Creek in Eight Days. Through Contracts will be made as soon as the condition of the road above Quesnelmouth permits.
Rates of Passage will be advertised in due time.

The first horseless carriage in Vancouver, an eight-seater made in 1899 at the Armstrong & Morrison ironworks and run by a steam engine heated by a gasoline burner.

By 1912 the automobile had caught on and cars were rallying at Ganges on Salt Spring Island (above) and providing Sunday jaunts for Cariboo people (below).

The people of Golden wheel into position
Captain Ernest Hoy's Canadian-built JN-4, in
which he made the first flight across the
Rockies in 1919. In the same year the first
airmail service was established into
Vancouver, from Seattle, U.S.A.

Mr. and Mrs. McIntosh Stark of Vancouver in
their Curtis flying machine.

# A Turn-of-the-Century Album

Part of the feeling of time arrested that comes from turn-of-the-century photographs is due to the processes of the period. People had to keep still for a minimum time — to pose, at least momentarily, as they would have done for a portrait. But in the case of British Columbians of that period, the feeling of a slower and perhaps a richer existence than ours was more than an affair of the camera shutter.

The tough pioneering days were over in much of the province, and the grinding mass poverty of the Late Victorian age was less evident on the Pacific Coast, since Montreal and Winnipeg had filtered out the poorest immigrants. Cities like Victoria and Vancouver, with their wooden mansions and their streets of small houses — each in its lawned and flowered lot — gave the visitor a sense of relative prosperity which tended to mask the islands of poverty and the recurrent social conflicts.

And, despite the periodic economic crises, people — at least until the end of the Edwardian era — had the sense of living in a peaceful world. All the threats of American invasion seemed securely in the past. Japan had neutralized Russia, and at this period Japan was Britain's friend. The Boer War had aroused a touch of patriotic fervour (a few hundred British Columbians had gone away to fight in South Africa, and some had died), but the conflict passed without leaving any more lasting trace on provincial life than a few streets named after Boer War generals and a few transported South African place names, like Ladysmith and Kimberley and Majuba Hill.

It was a world lacking in mechanical forms of entertainment: no cinema, no radio, no television. People depended largely on their own ingenuity to fill their leisure. Professional touring companies and well-known artists visited the theatres and opera houses in Vancouver and Victoria but rarely found their ways to smaller communities. Thus, music and the theatre, like sports, were largely amateur. The crowds — which were never large — went to see their fellow citizens performing, or else they amused themselves.

Much that went on in this way was still more British than in other parts of Canada. The tennis and croquet parties, the cricket games (only just beginning to give way in some interior towns to American sports like baseball), and the hunt clubs and garden parties were largely restricted to the middle class and were especially popular among the remittance men — the sons of wealthy British houses sent out to purge their indiscretions on small allowances transmitted from home, on condition that they never returned. But all classes enjoyed the band concerts and the public festivals on May Day and Victoria Day, and all shared the love of picnicking that was encouraged by the mild climate and abundant beaches and lakeshores.

The Hollow Tree has been a gathering point in Vancouver's Stanley Park ever since Lord Stanley opened the park in 1888. Some early Vancouverites entertain their guests there in 1891.

Mrs. Joseph Despard Pemberton, a Victoria matriarch, in her rose arbour.

A tennis party at the Goffin house in Victoria. The only man — whispering in the ear of Roberta Wolfenden — is G. E. Parkes.

The May Queen of New Westminster, with her maids of honour, about to begin her triumphal procession.

149

The orchestra and the dancing fairies at
Professor Wicker's annual concert in Victoria,
October 10, 1905.

Emily Carr with her animals in the garden of
the House of Small.

The Fatman's baseball team at Fernie.

The girls' hockey team in the Rossland
Skating Rink.

# The Reign of Glad-hand Dick

To the end of the nineteenth century British Columbian politicians tended to be federally Conservative (because the Tories were the party that built the railway) and provincially to follow their own patterns of factions based on local interest. But in the new century parties began to coalesce, with the Liberals organizing themselves in 1901 and the Conservatives in 1902; the election of 1903 was the first conducted on party lines, with Socialists competing as well as Liberals and Conservatives.

Undoubtedly, it was the emergence of the party system that led to the long ascendancy of Richard McBride. McBride was something of a boy wonder in western Canadian politics. In 1900, at the age of thirty, he became minister of mines in the government of James Dunsmuir. An affable, courtly man and something of a dandy, "Glad-hand Dick" made friends easily, in politics and outside, and for a long time he managed to convince a large number of the working men of British Columbia that he had their interests at heart.

Richard McBride as premier enjoyed an apotheosis in the columns of *The Week,* a pro-Tory magazine. In the March 16, 1912, issue he appears as a kind of Roi Soleil, with his leading opponents, Senator William Templeman and the future Liberal premiers Harlan Brewster and John Oliver, represented as the "blue-ruin brigade", blind to his glittering achievements.

The fishing fleet in the Fraser estuary during the great salmon run of 1905.

British Columbia's logging industry was made by hand; before the age of power saws, these fallers work from springboards to fell a first-growth Douglas fir with axe and handsaw.

Early logging locomotives in the coastal forests; they had not yet eliminated the need for horses.

By 1902, McBride realized that the Dunsmuir government was too shaky to survive, and, deserting the sinking ship at the opportune moment, he became leader of the Opposition, having physically to defend his appropriate seat in the legislature in a famous scuffle with the displaced leader, Joseph Martin. In 1903, McBride's Conservatives won the election, and at the age of thirty-three "the People's Dick", as his supporters also called him, became the youngest British Columbian premier. He survived in office until 1915 when he resigned, avoiding the Tory defeat of 1916. He guided the political destinies of the province longer than any later premier until W. A. C. Bennett started on his twenty-year term in 1952.

McBride was fortunate to preside over a period mostly of economic expansion. A number of phenomenal fish runs, in 1901 and 1905 particularly, pushed the canning industry into big business. Logging began to move into the interior and the more remote of the coastal inlets. Although the Oblate fathers had experimented with fruit growing in the Okanagan a generation before, it was during the early years of the twentieth century that the great orchard industry of that valley was developed, largely by English immigrants. Mixed farming was bringing the other valleys of the province into cultivation.

The cities were growing. Vancouver's population topped 110,000 in the 1911 census; Samuel Maclure was designing mansions and even mock castles in Victoria and the Shaughnessy Heights of Vancouver, while his rival F. M. Rattenbury built the Vancouver Courthouse and the Empress Hotel in Victoria. Suburbs began to cluster around centres less than a generation old. The urbanization of the Fraser Valley was preluded when the recently created transport and energy combine, the British Columbia Electric Company, pushed its interurban tramways up the Fraser Valley to Chilliwack.

This surge was based on the exploitation of natural resources in a way hitherto unparalleled in British Columbian history. American and, to a less extent, European capital flowed into the

The barque *Curzon* loads timber for Chile at Hastings Mill, Vancouver, in 1912.

F. M. Rattenbury's final gift to Victoria was the Empress Hotel, here shown shortly after completion. Opened in 1908, it initiated Victoria's career as a centre of tourism.

The prosperity of the McBride age was reflected in the fine houses erected in Vancouver and Victoria by Maclure, of which the most splendid was commissioned by James Dunsmuir, who had to rival his father by building an even larger "castle". Hatley Castle, overlooking Esquimalt Harbour, was completed in 1911; one hundred Chinese were employed as servants and as gardeners to tend the seven-hundred-acre estate.

province. By 1910, American investment in timber enterprises alone had reached $65 million, and the province has never freed itself from the alien economic domination established at this period. Land speculation, in Vancouver and also in remote areas of the province, reached new levels of rashness.

All this activity in so many directions was linked with another railway boom. During the first decade of the century two new transcontinental lines, the Grand Trunk Pacific and the Canadian Northern, were chartered and gained large land grants from the province. The first would go through the Yellowhead Pass and reach salt water at the mouth of the Skeena. The second would also use Yellowhead but would run south by the North Thompson to the Fraser, eventually terminating in Vancouver. And in 1912 yet another railway was announced, the Pacific Great Eastern, planned to connect Fort George to North Vancouver.

This multiple bonanza was what McBride offered to justify his long period in office. It made him more than a mere provincial politician; he was well regarded in Ottawa and was the only British Columbia premier ever knighted. Sir Richard could point to genuinely beneficial achievements, such as the first university in the province, stricter laws to conserve water and other resources, and some good labour and public health legislation.

Yet by the end of his reign the province was riven by labour discontent. A bitter strike in the Vancouver Island coal mines climaxed in August 1913 when strikers took over Nanaimo and turned their demonstration into a riot against Chinese and Japanese workers used to break the strike. William Bowser, attorney general and acting premier (McBride was absent in England), called out the militia, and for more than a year, until after World War I began, order in Nanaimo was maintained by armed troops. By such incidents the radical labour tradition of British Columbia was built up and sustained.

The British Columbia Electric Railway's interurban terminus at Chilliwack.

The railways in McBride's day were not only counters in great financial games; by providing a far more comfortable means of travel than ever before, they reflected the rapid rise in the accepted standard of life.

Granville Street, Vancouver, in 1912, facing
down to the first CPR station.

# Approach to the North

Until the very end of the nineteenth century, the northern parts of British Columbia remained unsettled. From the mid-1860s onward, prospectors passed through the country, and a series of rushes created fluid communities in the Omineca and Cassiar mining areas. But, in general, the pattern established by the North-westers in the early days of the century persisted; the permanent white population consisted of a few Hudson's Bay employees who traded with nomad Indians living a fairly traditional hunting life. In the far north of the province and on the Skeena and Nass rivers, even the fur traders did not make an appearance until the latter part of the century, since the inland trade was carried on by Tsimshian Indian middlemen; William Hankey, for example, reached the upper Skeena in 1868 to start direct trading for the Hudson's Bay Company. The Gitksan people of this region clung more obstinately to their traditions than any other British Columbian group of Indians, carrying on the potlatch in secret after it was forbidden in 1884 and raising totem poles (many of which still stand in their villages) well into the twentieth century. Their great hero was and remains the outlaw Simon Gun-an-noot, who in 1906 fled into the wilderness after he had been accused of murder, and eluded the police for thirteen years, surrendering voluntarily in the end.

Face of the North: a Gitksan carving at Kitwanga on the Skeena.

Hudson's Bay establishments, like the Fraser Lake post, remained virtually unchanged to the end of the nineteenth century.

Jean Caux — or Catiline as he was called for his Catalan ancestry — operated pack trains out of Hazelton from the turn of the century.

Simon Gun-an-Noot; the trial jury finally acquitted him.

William Hankey recognized the farming possibilities of the northern valleys and shortly after his arrival left the company's service to break land in the place he called Hazelton. Hazelton sprang into life as a community at the end of the 1890s when the Yukon Telegraph was established. Its position at the head of navigation on the Skeena made it a useful depot from which pack trains would set out to supply the telegraph constructors and operators, and also to transport supplies to the mines that still operated in the Omineca region.

But to most of the yet unoccupied northern region, life was brought by the coming of the Grand Trunk Pacific Railway, making its way through the valleys from Yellowhead Pass to the ocean. Plans were first announced by the Grand Trunk Pacific for its westward extension in 1903, but it was not until 1909 that arrangements were finally completed with the provincial government. In 1910, when construction had begun, a great speculative boom built up rapidly; timber licences were bought up throughout the region, and land speculators acquired tracts along the line of the railway. According to John Oliver, the Opposition leader, "the speculators sometimes get their land for a dollar and a drink and sometimes for a drink without the dollar."

However cheaply they bought, they sold at high prices. At Fort George in 1910 lots were selling for $10,000. Three town sites were plotted — Central Fort George and South Fort George as well as Fort George proper — but it was Fort George, where the railway company held most of the land, that became the new community (touted as "the railway hub of British Columbia"); in 1915 it was named Prince George.

Hazelton, round about 1910, with a pack train returning from the telegraph route.

Construction of the Grand Trunk Pacific, west of Yellowhead Pass.

While the railway was under construction, the mail was transported to Hazelton on rail trolleys pulled by dog teams.

It was balanced by Prince Rupert at the seaward end of the line, a brand-new town on Kaien Island which got its name by public competition; Prince Rupert had been the first governor of the Hudson's Bay Company in 1670. Thus, the two principal towns of northern British Columbia, as they have remained ever since, were brought into existence by the coming of the railway, which for the first time opened the northern timber lands, with their great stands of lumber and pulpwood, and also the rich fishing grounds off the province's northern coast, for which Prince Rupert became the centre.

Fort George in 1891, before the railway came.

The first white women arrive at Fort George in 1910, coming by paddle steamer up the Fraser from Quesnel.

The summer of the war! In July 1914 the grounds of Colonel Codd's residence on Rockland Avenue, Victoria, were filled with patriotic ladies and uniformed men attending the garden party for the IODE and the Gordon Highlanders, Vancouver's local volunteer regiment. Did they foresee what next month would bring?

## Wars and Rumours of Wars

The only wars that ever came to British Columbia (except for bush skirmishes with Indians, like the Chilcotin War and that grand and bloodless farce known as Ned McGowan's War) were fought far away, beyond the Rockies and beyond the vast expanse of Canada and the Atlantic Ocean. Yet, as the nineteenth century went on, the province became increasingly conscious of its vulnerability as one of the far-flung outposts of the Empire; it was also affected by Canada's growing sense of the need to undertake its own defence.

During the colonial years and for decades after Confederation, the main defence of British Columbia was provided by the Royal Navy, and the naval base at Esquimalt was the kingpin of the system. The Royal Engineers who arrived in 1858 were much more important for their contribution to the road system of the province and for the early public buildings they erected than for any military role they played, though they and the Royal Marines on the San Juan Islands provided a kind of deterrent to the expansionist ambitions of the Americans.

Perhaps they did. Volunteer enlistment in militia regiments had been increasing locally, and the Bay Street Armouries in Victoria were under construction when war began.

But when the Royal Navy went into action in Burrard Inlet on July 23, 1914, it was against British, not German, subjects as the *Komagata Maru* with its hundreds of would-be immigrants was shown out of Canadian waters.

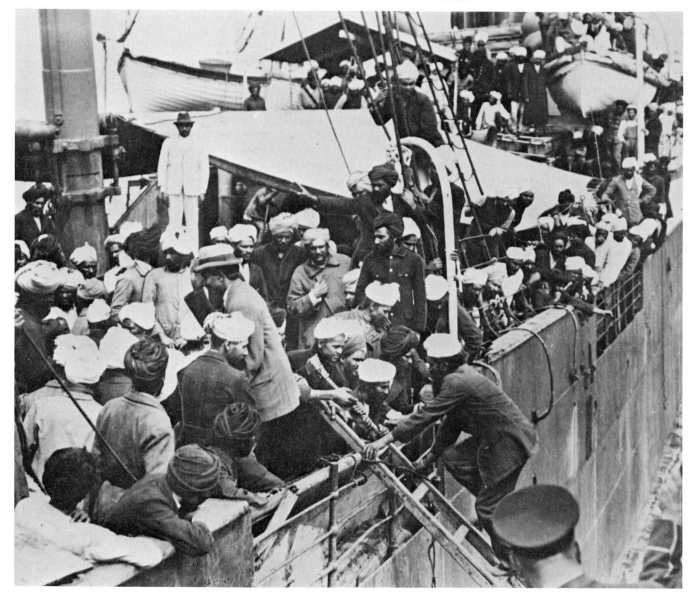

Commanding the Gordon Highlanders was Lieutenant-Colonel A. W. Currie, a Sidney real estate agent and land speculator who eventually rose to the rank of general and succeeded Sir Julian Byng in command of the Canadian Corps.

On Christmas Day 1914 the CPR ferry boat *Princess Victoria,* transformed into a military transport, left Victoria with a cargo of recruits on their way to Europe.

The fortifications at Esquimalt were defended, not by Canadians but by three hundred men of the Royal Marine Artillery and the Royal Engineers. But from 1887 a regular detachment of Canadian artillery was stationed on Beacon Hill, and from 1897 the Canadian government shared in the cost of the Esquimalt garrison. In 1878, during the Russian war scare, earthworks were hurriedly built on the approaches to Esquimalt and Victoria, and in the 1890s, when fears were being aroused by the growing naval power of Germany and Japan, modern fortifications were constructed and equipped with the latest in 6-inch disappearing guns and 12-inch quick-firing guns.

The Anglo-Japanese alliance of 1904 resulted in a reorganization of Royal Navy fleet arrangements by which in 1905 Esquimalt ceased to be headquarters of the Pacific station. Only the dockyard and bunkering facilities were maintained, and in 1906 the British garrison departed and Canadian troops took over. In 1910, when Sir Wilfrid Laurier's government created a separate Royal Canadian Navy, the dockyards were finally handed to Canada. The cruiser *Rainbow* was stationed at Esquimalt and went into action less than a month before the war began — not against a naval enemy but to escort out of Vancouver Harbour the freighter *Komagata Maru,* which arrived with 376 prospective Sikh immigrants, all British subjects, who were declared inadmissible by the Canadian authorities; they had repelled with a fusillade of coal the force of 175 police and immigration officers who tried to board the ship.

The *Komagata Maru* was sent away on July 23. Less than two weeks later, on August 4, Britain declared war on Germany, and Canada, without debating the matter, became a belligerent. During the immediately preceding years there had been a considerable militia build-up in British Columbia; in 1912 training grounds for mounted troops had been established at Vernon in the Okanagan Valley, and work had started on armouries like that on Bay Street in Victoria, commenced in 1913. Psychologically, as well, the British Columbians, and particularly the many of British birth, were prepared for the war, and the militia units mobilized quickly. By August 26 the first detachments from Victoria and the mainland left for Valcartier; by October 1 more than three thousand British Columbians had sailed for Britain. Among them was Lieutenant-Colonel Arthur W. Currie of the Gordon Highlanders, who eventually commanded the Canadian Corps. Altogether, British Columbia, with a population somewhat over 400,000, contributed 55,000 men to the armed forces. More than 43,000 served overseas, 6,225 were killed, and more than 13,000 were wounded. Most of the recruits went east by rail, but in 1918, after the Russian revolution, a detachment sailed from Vancouver to join the Allied force in Siberia.

The strangest story of the war was the three-day existence of a British Columbian navy. It was known, when the war began, that the German cruisers *Leipzig* and *Nürnberg* were patrolling the Pacific; they might attack British Columbia. Premier McBride, anxious for his province and impatient at the weakness

On a rainy March day of 1916 the 62nd Overseas Battalion entrains for overseas service at Hastings Park siding.

of naval defences, heard that two submarines had been completed by a Seattle shipyard for the Chilean government. Before receiving permission from higher authorities, he bought them with $1,150,000 of provincial funds. For three days after this high-handed act without consent of the legislature, the submarines remained the property of British Columbia; on August 7 they were handed over to the dominion, which donated them to the British Admiralty.

Although none of the war was fought on British Columbian soil or off its coasts, it brought about profound changes in the province's life. Women were given the vote, Mrs. Mary Ellen Smith sat as a member in the provincial legislature, and the first woman judge presided over a juvenile court in Vancouver. Large areas of the province were greatly changed. Mines in the interior were exhausted by the demand for copper; Phoenix and Greenwood became ghost towns. Nobody went back to tend the orchards at Walhachin near Kamloops, whose British settlers had left the day war was declared. Labour had become more aggressive; on August 21, 1918, a twenty-four-hour general strike was held to protest the shooting of a militant miner. Returned soldiers clashed with unionists, but socialism was spreading and for the first time attracting a large proportion of British Columbians. There was an undercurrent of apprehension to the rejoicings of November 11, 1918.

Traffic draws to a halt on Cambie Street as a military parade follows the band down Hastings Street, Vancouver.

The end of the war in Europe did not mean
the end of military involvement for Canadians.
In 1918 the Siberian Expeditionary Force
sailed on the transport *Monteagle* from
Vancouver to Vladivostock; it was not
withdrawn until the following year.

# Academic Vicissitudes

One of the casualties of World War I in British Columbia was higher education, which in 1914 was just beginning to get into its stride. There had been schools in British Columbia since 1854, when the colonial government of Vancouver Island established Craigflower School, the first school west of Lake Superior in what is now Canada. Five years later the Colonial School was established in Victoria. These schools were subsidized by the colonial government, but parents were still expected to pay fees, and there were also unsubsidized private schools for those with social pretensions, as well as schools patronized by the Church of England and the Roman Catholic Church.

Education in these early days was subject to the succession of booms and depressions that marked a gold-mining economy, and only a few communities ventured public funds on schools. By 1872 the public schools of Victoria were actually closed down for lack of funds. In 1876, when the economic situation seemed brighter, the era of one-room schools finally seemed near its end with the construction of the Central School in Victoria, with more than seven hundred registered students, but by 1879 the school was running into debt and a special poll tax had to be levied to keep it going.

In education, as in other respects, the completion of the CPR changed the situation in British Columbia. The towns which the railway sprouted — like Vancouver and, to a less extent, Kamloops and Revelstoke — grew rapidly in importance, while in general the provincial economy was stimulated and population increased. High schools appeared in Vancouver, Victoria, Esquimalt, and other towns.

In 1890 the Act for the creation of a provincial university was passed by the Legislative Assembly, and Premier John Robson picked Dr. Israel Wood Powell, an associate of Amor De Cosmos in the struggle for Confederation, as first chancellor.

Craigflower School, built in 1854, the first publicly operated school in British Columbia.

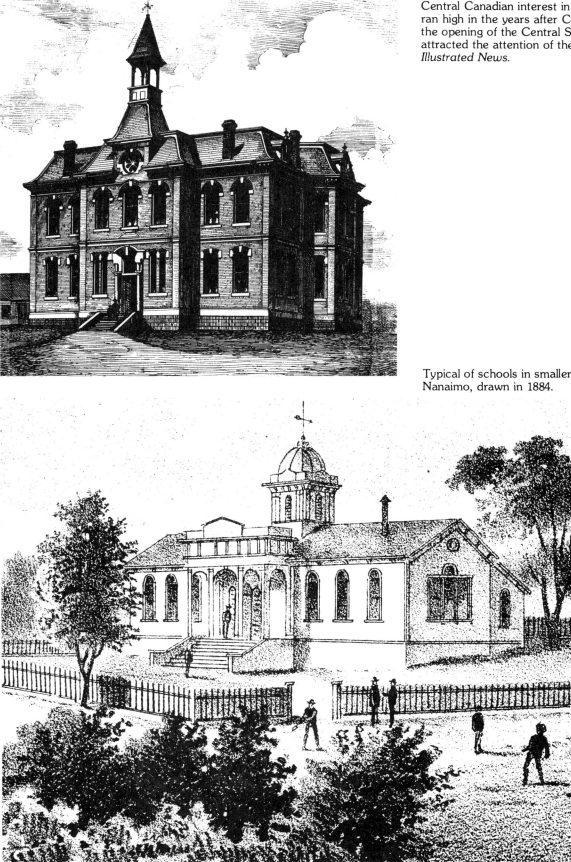

Central Canadian interest in British Columbia ran high in the years after Confederation, and the opening of the Central School in Victoria attracted the attention of the *Canadian Illustrated News*.

Typical of schools in smaller towns was that in Nanaimo, drawn in 1884.

During the Great Trek of October 28, 1922, the protesting students gather around the skeleton of the Science Building on which work was begun nine years earlier and then abandoned.

The Normal School in Victoria, opened in 1914. Later the building was used by Victoria College.

However, a dispute between Victoria and Vancouver interests over the location of the university rendered the legislation dormant, and for the time being other ways were found of providing the modest amount of higher education the province could sustain. In 1899 the Vancouver High School was affiliated to McGill University, as was Victoria College, founded in 1903 in a two-room building in the grounds of Victoria High School. These establishments merely carried on a two-year freshman and sophomore program until, in 1913, the University of British Columbia, still a branch of McGill, began to operate in the Fairview Shacks overlooking False Creek while the site finally chosen at Point Grey was prepared. Construction at Point Grey began in 1914 but was abandoned when the war began, though construction was completed on the Victoria Normal School, which opened in 1914. Still lacking any usable buildings on its campus, the University of British Columbia was chartered as an independent foundation in 1915. Victoria College was absorbed into the new university, which immediately lost to the army a fifth of its three hundred students.

By 1920 the failure of the provincial government to resume its building program led to such overcrowding in the Fairview huts that Victoria College again became a two-year establishment affiliated to the university, operating from Craigdarroch Castle and later from the Normal School. It took the big student demonstration of 1922, known in academic annals as the Great Trek, to alert the Liberal government of John Oliver to the need to resume work on the skeletons of buildings that had stood waiting for completion at Point Grey for the past nine years. In 1923 funds were allocated which enabled the nucleus of the present campus to be built.

The second CPR station in Vancouver, built just before World War I, was a fine example of the kind of railway-baroque architecture that found its most notable expression in New York's Pennsylvania Railroad Station.

## Cities Under Siege

The years between the great wars were a time of varied fortunes for British Columbia's cities, which for quite long periods lived under a kind of economic siege. Immediately after the armistice the economy was jolted by the sudden fall in the demand for raw materials, and particularly metals, which had been stimulated by the war. The demobilization of the tens of thousands of soldiers who had survived the war combined with the constriction of industry to produce widespread unemployment, and it was only slowly that Vancouver and the mainland interior emerged into an upswing that continued from 1922 until the end of the 1920s; this was stimulated by increased exports of forest products by way of the Panama Canal, opened in August 1914, and also by the development of Vancouver as a port, particularly for shipping prairie wheat.

But there was nothing resembling the prewar boom of 1906-13, and many projects that had been touted in the years before the war did not reach fruition. The Grand Trunk Pacific, drifting into bankruptcy, had been taken over by the federal government and eventually became part of the Canadian National, while the Pacific Great Eastern, which in 1914 McBride had prophesied would reach Alaska, ended as a truncated line between two villages — starting at Quesnel in the Cariboo,

The urge to renew and expand that was part of the spirit of the early 1920s led the department chains to enlarge and embellish their stores into city landmarks, like the new Hudson's Bay store which in 1921 was opened in Victoria.

whence it ran down through the ranching country and the Coast Mountains to end at Squamish; hence a ferry carried passengers down Howe Sound to Vancouver.

And if Vancouver prospered and grew until the depression slowed down the economy in every direction at the end of the 1920s, Victoria remained so stagnant economically that between the two censuses of 1921 and 1931 the city's population grew by only three hundred. Greater Vancouver, by contrast, had by the middle of the twenties passed the quarter of a million mark.

Yet, throughout this period, booming or stagnating, the cities changed in appearance. Building went on, and in Vancouver the suburbs of new houses spread into districts like Kerrisdale and Burnaby that had remained woodland or had been used as truck gardens. On January 1, 1929, the city boundaries were broadened and the municipalities of South Vancouver and Point Grey were absorbed, so that Vancouver now stretched from Burrard Inlet to the Fraser River.

In both larger cities the department stores extended their premises and dominated more of the retail trade. Movie theatres appeared, and live theatre began to wither, while, as everywhere in Canada, the radio programs (which from 1936 onward came from the CBC) began to play an important part in people's lives and to diminish the inclination to rely on one's own initiative or creativity for amusement. World War I saw the final triumph of the automobile and the rapid disappearance of horse traffic from

the city streets. And the mood of the twenties, here as else-where, showed itself in the extremities of fashion, in the desire for more amusement and more leisure, in the elaborate devices by which the strict liquor regulations which replaced prohibition at the beginning of the 1920s were evaded to preserve social amenities (so that the bootlegger remained a feature of the British Columbian scene), and by the easing of the housewife's tasks through such developments as the spread of refrigeration and the flood of labour-saving devices which the newly expanded department stores began to offer.

Even the rigours of the depression did not entirely negate these developments, at least in the cities, where people who had money lived better because of falling prices, even if those who had nothing were pushed to the edge of survival. By the end of the thirties the first signs of economic recovery were appearing, and there were bizarre conjunctions. In 1938 Vancouver was scarred by demonstrations and riots, but in the same year the Lion's Gate Bridge was built, spanning Burrard Inlet to open the North Shore to prosperous residential development.

Opposite above: In the heart of downtown Vancouver, on the corner of Granville and Georgia streets, the Hudson's Bay windows charted the vagaries of fashion. A window in 1923, draped entirely with purple velour, announced a campaign for ten thousand new customers; the times were still expansive.

Opposite below: A few months later, a Spring Opening window introduced the current styles of 1924; the flapper age had come with discretion to Vancouver.

The triumph of the automobile had transformed law enforcement. In 1927, motor-cycle cops posed outside Vancouver's police station with one of the Moreland trucks whose fast international services were part of the postwar revolution in transport.

A Granville Street trolley heads for Kitsilano,
already a well-established residential area. The
facades of the buildings suggest the
eclecticism of Vancouver architecture. No two
are in the same tradition.

Victoria's architecture between the wars was even more traditional than Vancouver's. Christ Church Cathedral was built in impressive Gothic Revival during the 1920s (left), and the Royal Oak Inn (now the Maltwood Art Museum) in a harmonious neo-Tudor during the 1930s (below).

Up to the end of the 1930s West Vancouver was linked directly to Vancouver only by ferry. In 1938 the Lion's Gate Bridge (shown in a modern photograph) was completed across Burrard Inlet, and a development of the North Shore mountainsides began in the expensive British Properties residential suburb with its beautiful summer views and its icy steep roads in winter.

# Honest John, the Farmer's Friend

The time that bridged the two wars was the final stage of old-line party politics in British Columbia. It began in 1916 when the Conservatives, deprived of their long-time leader Sir Richard McBride, were defeated under his successor William Bowser, and the Liberal government of Harlan C. Brewster took office. It ended in 1941 when Duff Pattullo's Liberal government collapsed and the period of coalition rule that lasted until 1952 began.

John Oliver (who took over as premier when Brewster died in 1918 and held office until 1927) and Duff Pattullo (who became premier in 1933 and resigned in 1941) were perhaps the most vigorous Liberal leaders the province has known. The Tory government of Dr. Simon Fraser Tolmie that intervened between their administrations was undistinguished at best and was destroyed by its own inability to deal with the problems of the depression.

The Liberals took office in 1916 with a large majority (thirty-seven of them against nine Tories) on a reform platform. Brewster gave votes to the women (which they exercised in the 1920 elections), established a Ministry of Labour, and passed the province's first Minimum Wages Act. His successor John Oliver, who had started life as a pit boy in Derbyshire and had become a Fraser Valley farmer, was the first of a number of populist premiers of British Columbia, concerned especially with exploiting agricultural possibilities and making farming more attractive in a province unhealthily dominated by primary exploitative industries like timber, minerals, and fishing.

Under Oliver's leadership the Liberal government provided for the draining of Sumas Lake in the Fraser Valley and the great marshes surrounding it, and dairy farms appeared where early travellers reported being driven away by clouds of aggressive mosquitoes. Among those who settled this new land were Mennonite farmers who had fled from Soviet Russia. The Liberals also undertook the irrigation of the arid southern end of the Okanagan Valley, and the fruit-growing town which sprang up there was named Oliver in the premier's honour. Oliver introduced a Produce Marketing Act that protected the prices which the Okanagan orchardists got for their fruit. And he negotiated the return of the rich square of northern farmland known as the Peace River Block, which the province had transferred to the dominion in 1884 as part of the terms for the Canadian Pacific Railway's completion. Settlers began to go there even before World War I, and during the depression years many more were to arrive after abandoning the drought-stricken dirt farms of southern Saskatchewan.

Oliver's government completed the purchase by the province of the Pacific Great Eastern Railway, built many roads, and introduced the first old age pensions legislation anywhere in Canada. Circumstances favoured Honest John, as his followers

"Honest" John Oliver's nickname seemed to be borne out by the dour rectitude his face assumed towards the end of his life: just but joyless.

The element of exuberant defiance that was also part of Oliver's character is caught — in a style of drawing reminiscent of Toulouse-Lautrec — by the caricaturist George Hagen.

Hagen also caught, in the puffy and petulant features, the essence of Oliver's great opponent, the Tory leader William Bowser.

One of the main areas of new agricultural development encouraged by John Oliver's government was the Peace River country, where in the 1930s the pioneer farmers built St. Peter's Church at Hudson's Hope.

called him, for by the middle twenties it seemed as though the hinterland of the province, from which he drew his political strength, would return to the prosperity of McBride's days. In 1926 the production of both minerals and fish reached record dollar values, the output of pulp and paper was high, and the British Columbia Electric Company had embarked on a large hydro-electric development at Bridge River north of Lillooet.

But reform governments are particularly susceptible to discontent, on the right because they seem to go too fast, on the left because they do not go fast enough. A right-wing revolt of disaffected Liberals and Tories, centred in the business quarters of Vancouver, produced the Provincial Party which contested the 1924 elections so vigorously that, though they elected only three representatives, they reduced Liberal votes and left Oliver to govern precariously with twenty-four members in a house of forty-eight — which meant that he had to rely on the votes of Independents and the Labour members who represented a growing social-democratic trend related to the persistent militancy of the labour unions.

Like so many British Columbian premiers, Oliver died in office. His successor John D. MacLean had little of his predecessor's populist spirit. After an unimaginative year in power, when nothing was done to implement the health insurance schemes Oliver had proposed, MacLean called an election in which the currents of discontent ran together to sweep away the Liberals and return the Tories, under Dr. Tolmie, with a large majority. As it turned out, the Liberals benefited from their defeat, for in just over a year the stock market crashed in New York and the good days came to an end all over North America.

John Oliver's draining of Sumas Lake added many needed acres to the scanty arable land of British Columbia and made possible the development of dairy farms like this one. But it also destroyed one of the great North American halting places for migratory waterfowl.

Vast areas of British Columbia have always been too dry or too soilless for cultivation, and this has meant that in many areas, like the Nicola region, ranching has been the main occupation with the cattle drive a great annual event.

A pre-depression boom in logging was one of the features of John Oliver's time. Logging railways found their way through the hinterland, as in Bloedel, Stewart and Welsh's operation at Myrtle Point in this 1926 photograph.

Camps where large numbers of men lived in bunk houses sprang up in the wilderness, like the Merrill and Ring camp on Theodosia Arm. When the forests were felled around them, they vanished as quickly as the miners' ghost towns.

Steam donkey engines dragging logs through the woods on highlines were a feature of logging at this period. Note the special chimney to minimize risks of sparks flying out to start forest fires.

# Depression, Class War, and World War

Dr. Simon Fraser Tolmie was an excellent veterinarian and cattle breeder, and he had served efficiently as minister of agriculture in Conservative federal governments, led during the early postwar years by Robert Borden and Arthur Meighen. He appealed to British Columbians largely because his father, William Fraser Tolmie, had been a Hudson's Bay chief factor in the 1840s and a personal associate of Sir James Douglas. More than any other politician of the time, he seemed to incarnate a tradition that had remained British Columbian without becoming irrevocably Canadian.

But his qualifications were not of a kind that made him capable of dealing with a depression whose larger causes operated beyond the Rocky Mountains and, indeed, beyond the frontiers of Canada. Owing to the glut in the world grain market, the export of wheat, on which the port of Vancouver so largely depended, declined sharply. The coastal and interior regions of the province were more directly affected by the rapidly falling international demand for British Columbian lumber and canned fish. Commerce went into retreat and business houses into bankruptcy. By 1929 the first breadlines began to appear in Vancouver, where by the spring of 1930 some 7,000 men were on relief. By February 1932 there were more than 67,000 unemployed in a province whose population according to the 1931 census was 694,000. By 1933 the figure had reached 100,000, or somewhat more than one in eight of the population; it was swollen by unemployed men who had ridden the rods from eastern Canada and the prairie provinces in search of a climate where malnutrition might be more endurable.

Unemployed men in the mid-1930s walk in ragged procession along Granville Street's sidewalk while the police keep them off the roadway. In many ways, the scene typified one side of British Columbian life during the depression, especially in Vancouver with its large shifting population of migrant workless.

But in the rural areas people like these northern cowboys, photographed in the summer of 1934, often withdrew into traditional ways of living by the land and reverted largely to a barter economy in which cash circulated slowly.

Tolmie's Conservative government had little to offer but a program of budgetary restraint which — among other things — cut the university's scanty budget by 43 per cent and had the general effect of further restricting the opportunities of employment. Beyond economy, all Tolmie could think of was an all-party coalition as a kind of magic panacea, but Duff Pattullo — as Liberal leader — rejected the proposal, and so did the leaders of the newly founded Co-operative Commonwealth Federation, the CCF, Canada's first mass social-democratic party that united both labour and farm interests under the same party banner. When an election was called in 1933, the Tories were so routed that only three of them retained seats in the legislature. The Liberals, with thirty-four seats, had more than a comfortable majority. But the most significant feature of the election was that the new entrants in the contest, the CCF, though they won only seven seats (enough to make them the official Opposition) gleaned 31 per cent — or almost a third — of the popular vote.

Pattullo, a somewhat theatrical dandy, was also a man of intelligence and genuine concern for the sufferings of people who had been deprived of their livelihood by a depression that made other people prosperous. He developed into a kind of British Columbian New Dealer (he greatly admired F. D. Roosevelt), willing to spend the province's way out of disaster. He and his minister of finance, John Hart, deliberately budgeted for deficits and started a project of public works, of which the most spectacular was the Pattullo Bridge at New Westminster, begun in 1935 and ended in 1937, which not only gave much employment but also vastly improved the transport links between Greater Vancouver, the Fraser Valley, and the American border.

Among the Indians of the province's northland, the depression had little effect. They were poor in any case, and in cash terms they merely became slightly poorer. But they had not yet lost their skills as hunters and fishermen, and as the well-made dugout canoe seen here suggests, their life was still largely traditional in spite of their white men's clothes.

One of the more sensational episodes of the 1930s was the Bédaux expedition, which attempted to cross unmapped territory between Edmonton and the Alaska panhandle. The country defeated Bédaux's half-tracks, which he had used successfully in the Sahara and the Central African jungle, and the expedition escaped from the wilderness by water. Here they raft down the Halfway River in August 1934.

It was a period of sharply rising discontent, for Pattullo's measures merely scratched the surface of the problems. In 1935 the demonstrations of the unemployed in Vancouver became so threatening that Mayor Gerry McGeer found it necessary to read the Riot Act; in 1938 the demonstrators demanding better treatment for single workless men occupied the post office and other public buildings, and rioted in the streets, causing a good deal of damage to property; they were brutally expelled by the RCMP and the city police.

The surge of disgust with existing parties and leaders found expression in political radicalism. It ranged from the communism professed by many leaders of the unemployed (and the Trotskyism of a few) to the democratic socialism embodied in the CCF, which sustained its strength in successive elections and in 1941 elected fourteen members of the Legislative Assembly and polled 33 per cent of the popular vote.

This success of the CCF, which made that party the official Opposition in a wartime government, marked the end of the system of rule by alternating Conservative and Liberal parties. The Liberals at best could form a minority government with their twenty-one elected members, and the party membership rebelled from Pattullo's leadership to conclude an alliance with the Conservatives which led to a professedly antisocialist coalition government; under John Hart and later "Boss" Johnson, it ruled the province until the early 1950s.

World War II did not levy the same kind of toll on British Columbian manpower as its predecessor. More men joined the armed forces; far fewer were killed or wounded in proportion to the total. But the wartime demand for materials revived every one of British Columbia's flagging industries, turned the province temporarily into a shipbuilding centre, and, as a result of the building of the Alaska Highway in 1942, united the Peace River country effectively with the province and opened the mining regions of the far north near the Yukon border.

The most visible of Pattullo's public works to relieve unemployment was the bridge that bears his name and links Vancouver and New Westminster with the lower Fraser Valley. The strange-looking structure in mid-river is the bascule of the open swing bridge carrying the railway; the stern-wheeler is the Samson, used for removing snags and floating logs that imperilled navigation.

In June 1935, strikers from the work camps
for unemployed men in the interior of British
Columbia boarded freight trains at Kamloops,
intending to demonstrate at Ottawa. They
were halted in Regina, which led to the
disturbances known as the Regina Riots.

Vancouver unemployed demonstrate for work
and collect funds at the same time.

Sit-in demonstrators in 1938, beaten by the police as they leave the Vancouver General Post Office.

Some of the men who took part in Vancouver demonstrations were also present in that curtain raiser to World War II, the Spanish Civil War. Even before the Mac-Paps were formed, these Canadians had joined the American Lincoln Battalion in the International Brigade.

With their wives and children following them,
the men of the British Columbia Regiment
march down to the docks at New Westminster
to embark for Europe and the war.

In 1939 the main defences of British Columbia were still the batteries at Fort Rodd outside Esquimalt, built in the 1890s. They were finally abandoned in 1956.

Among the ships built in British Columbia during World War II was the corvette *Edmonston*, launched at Esquimalt in 1941.

# Awakening from Depression and War

Wars are great agents of change, often for the worse but sometimes for the better. True, there were some respects in which British Columbia seemed little changed as it shook free from the Second World War. The towns had not altered greatly, for there had been little building during the war and not a great deal during the 1930s. The great steam locomotives of the past still toiled their way through the passes of the Rockies; the neat black-and-white Canadian Pacific ferry boats provided the main connection with Vancouver Island; the old wooden mansions of Edwardian days still rotted beside the streets of Vancouver's West End, and the middle-class housing in the new suburbs of the 1920s was looking shabby from years of neglect; a decade and a half of municipal cheese-paring had left the cities with obsolete public transportation, inadequate sewage and water systems, old schools in need of repair, and parks in need of attention. The Cariboo Road was still unpaved, and the only Canadian highway through the Selkirks — the only way from Vancouver to Calgary except by American territory — was little better than a track around the Big Bend of the Columbia. It was a familiar world worn out by a succession of crises to which the men and women came back from the wars.

A CPR passenger train winds down through the Rockies at Field in the last days of steam.

Powell River: the town and MacMillan Bloedel's pulp mill.

An oil exploration rig in northern British Columbia during the early 1950s.

The Sullivan Mine at Kimberley, which for almost ninety years has been producing metallic ores for the Trail smelter. There is still no end in sight to its riches.

But the wars, which had left so much in the cities to decay, had already created the means by which the province would be renewed by opening the north country with the building of the Alaska Highway and a little later of the Hart Highway that linked the Peace River with the Cariboo Road and so with Vancouver.

Exploration for oil and natural gas began, and by the early 1950s the first oil pipeline was being built over the mountains from Alberta. A new industrial development started up in the province's hinterland, based on a more intensive exploitation of natural resources. The presence of abundant hydro power led Alcan to build its great aluminum plant at Kitimat on a formerly deserted inlet on the northern coast of British Columbia. New sawmills and pulp mills appeared on Vancouver Island, in the Kootenays, in Prince George, and the pulp mill at Powell River was greatly enlarged, as was the great Cominco smelting plant at Trail. Industrial concentration became more pronounced as small sawmills were forced out of business and as the number of fish canneries fell to a sixth of those in operation thirty years before. Industrial parks appeared on the edges of British

Trail: the modern smelter with its subsidiary industries.

Pouring slag at the Trail smelter.

197

Grant McConachie, one of Canada's famous bush pilots, was among the moving spirits in the formation of CP Air from a dozen local competing outfits. Later he became CP Air's president.

From 1942 onwards, CP Air was flying DC-3s along the coast and among the islands. By the 1950s it was probing southward to Mexico, Peru, and Argentina, and eastward to Japan.

Columbian towns and in former waste places like Annacis Island in the Fraser River, and here new secondary industries began to operate.

The burgeoning of industry led to massive shifts in population and to a rapid growth of residential building. By 1947 Vancouver had increased in population to 340,000, and this meant that the old buildings of the city began to give way to modern apartment and office blocks, while new housing estates colonized the hitherto sparsely populated North Shore and clambered up the mountainsides above Burrard Inlet. To serve the new factories and suburbs, hydro-electric projects were being constructed in many parts of the province by the British Columbia Electric Company and the publicly owned British Columbia Power Commission which had been founded in 1945 to provide better electric supplies to the more remote areas of the province. And, to meet expanding transport needs, airlines began to lace the hinterland together on a scale unknown before, from small bush lines going into the remote interior and serving distant coastal points to the great new enterprise, Canadian Pacific Airlines, which aimed to rival the publicly owned TCA and was centred on Vancouver.

It was in this atmosphere of mounting development that British Columbians decided to shake off their old political system, represented by the decaying Liberal-Conservative coalition. In 1952 the electors swept it out of the way to make room for rule by a new party and a little-known leader.

At Kitimat the site for a great aluminum plant and a city of 13,500 people to serve it was carved out of the wilderness between 1951 and 1954 by the Aluminum Company of Canada.

Premier Bennett, acting as his own finance minister, delivers the 1962 budget speech in the marbled solemnity of the Legislative Assembly.

# The Long Reign of Wacky Bennett

In 1952 populism took over power in British Columbia, and in right-wing and left-wing forms it has controlled the province ever since, to the apparently permanent exclusion of the old Liberal and Conservative parties. The Liberal-Conservative coalition had been established to fend off the threat of socialism, but when it broke off at the beginning of the 1950s it was an entirely new movement, headed by a hinterland politician who had never held office before, that emerged as the most powerful political force.

This was Social Credit, which in 1949 had contested the provincial election and gained a mere 1.5 per cent of the popular vote. Social Credit's fortunes changed because it coalesced with a movement of grass roots discontent that had been building up around the figure of W. A. C. Bennett, an Okanagan hardware merchant and MLA who had twice, in 1946 and 1950, tried for the leadership of the Conservative party. Not only was Bennett defeated on both occasions, but he was consistently passed over

In the early days of Bennett's rule, the economy of the province was already moving forward rapidly. The Alcan plant at Kitimat went into operation, and out of its pot-rooms 270,000 tonnes of aluminum per annum would eventually emerge.

In 1957 Westcoast Transmission brought its natural gas pipeline down through the mountains to the lower mainland.

Work begins on the extension of the Pacific Great Eastern (later to become the British Columbia Railway) at North Vancouver.

when appointments to the Cabinet were made. In 1951 he withdrew from the coalition, became an independent, and began to gather around him a movement of those who were discontented with the way the coalition had centred on Vancouver and Victoria, ignoring not only the rural districts but also the urban lower-middle class.

Thus, a parallel confrontation was established to the traditional West Coast conflict between militant labour and the tough primary industrialists with their political associates. Now it was the forgotten men of the middle classes, farmers and small-business men, clerks and professionals, who were in revolt, and when Bennett joined Social Credit the movement spread so fast that the 1952 election became a vast demonstration against the old establishment. Social Credit won nineteen seats and the CCF eighteen, and together they polled more than 64 per cent of the popular vote; the outsiders had risen. The old parties shared ten seats between them. Bennett formed a minority government and in an election the following year gained a majority, with twenty-eight seats and a popular vote of 45.5 per cent; by now the old parties between them shared a mere 24 per cent of the vote.

Social Credit in British Columbia has never stood for the monetary reform measures that originally distinguished the

With the completion of the Trans-Canada Highway through Rogers Pass in the Selkirks, an effective all-Canadian route from British Columbia to the rest of Canada was at last established.

movement, though it has sustained its populist image by gifts to the populace like free hospital care and remissions of house taxes and by a simulated toughness towards big industry. Bennett raised provincial levies on mining and logging, and in 1961 he actually stole a march on the socialists by taking over the British Columbia Electric Company and turning it into the publicly owned British Columbia Hydro and Power Authority.

But Social Credit has never been socialist in the broader sense, and Bennett, with the characteristic grandiosity that earned him the nickname of "Wacky Bennett", devoted himself mostly to establishing the physical infrastructure of an industrial economy aimed at the maximum exploitation of natural resources. Railways and roads were always high on his agenda. In 1954 the extension of the Pacific Great Eastern to Fort St. John and Peace River in the north and to North Vancouver in the south was begun; by 1971 the railway was extended beyond Fort St. John to Fort Nelson near the Yukon Territory (which Bennett coveted as part of a greater British Columbia), and so the two extremities of the province were at last united. Bennett also pushed ahead in 1954 the completion of the lagging British Columbian part of the Trans-Canada Highway, setting up a special Department of Highways under the flamboyant

Two eras of road building. The original
Alexandra Bridge on the Cariboo Road is in
the foreground, and in the background the
new Alexandra Bridge built when the Social
Credit government turned the road into part
of the Trans-Canada Highway.

The British Columbia Electric headquarters,
designed by Ron Thom, was one of the most
advanced Vancouver buildings of the 1950s.
With the takeover of British Columbia Electric
in 1961, it became headquarters of the publicly
owned British Columbia Hydro and Power
Authority.

Geologists at the site of the Bennett Dam, examining dinosaur relics.

The Bennett Dam channelled the forces of the Peace River to further the Social Credit's plans for distributing hydro power more widely in British Columbia.

Pentecostal revivalist Phil Gaglardi, which in 1959 announced a billion-dollar road construction program spread over ten years. By the end of W. A. C. Bennett's rule in 1972, every British Columbian community of the least importance was served by a paved highway.

The industries springing up along the new roads and railways also needed power, as did the ordinary people of the hinterland on whom Bennett depended for his basic vote. A widespread program of rural electrification was accompanied by the building of great dams on the Peace River and the Columbia which are probably the most massive monuments to the Bennett era. But there were other achievements. A publicly owned ferry fleet was established. New universities and colleges were built. And, as a symbol of a provincialism that at times sounded like incipient separatism, a Bank of British Columbia was created.

A historian has called Wacky Bennett and his government "the New Romans". Like the Romans, they indeed built monumentally, and like them they tended in the end to lose sight of the human scale, so that by the early 1970s they had benefited industry greatly but had created as many areas of discontent — among teachers, among unionists, among the poor — as the old parties had done twenty years before.

In 1972 a political era came to an end when the NDP (as the CCF had become) finally leapt out of its long apprenticeship as official Opposition and under Dave Barrett, a populist of the left, defeated Bennett, the populist of the right, and took over the government of the province. The electoral positions of the past two decades were dramatically reversed. The NDP took thirty-eight seats, Social Credit ten, and the old parties seven between them. But there was a difference between 1952 and 1972. Social Credit was too deeply rooted in the hopes and fears of the middle class to die away as the old parties had done. It survived to fight another day.

The Celgar Pulp Mill at Castlegar was one of the later industrial projects under the Bennett regime, using power from Columbia River hydro developments to process wood from the forests of the Kootenays.

Under Social Credit the provincial economy continued to be highly exploitative of natural resources. A Canadian Pacific train carries coal from the Kaiser strip-mining project in the East Kootenays to a new port opened in 1970 at Roberts Bank south of Vancouver, for shipment to Japan.

W. A. C. Bennett grins triumphantly for the cameras at the inauguration of a PGE railway extension north of Prince George.

# Academies and Artifacts

The great physical changes that took place in British Columbia during the Bennett era were paralleled by cultural changes only partly linked with the political complexion of the period. Like those of every other province of Canada, the educational needs of British Columbia expanded through a rapid increase in child population, a radical transformation of educational expectations, and great changes in society's professional and technological needs. A far larger proportion of students expected to proceed from high school to university, and the range of knowledge available to them simultaneously increased.

The Bennett government recognized that on the primary level a situation had arisen which could not be met by the old system of school boards operating with local taxes, and in 1954 the Public Schools Construction Act was passed, which committed the province to sharing in the cost of new schools and led to the virtual extinction of the little white clapboard schoolhouse of the West as primary and secondary education was consolidated in large establishments, supplied (as it were) by widespread school bus services.

Simon Fraser University started Arthur Erickson on his career as an internationally known architect. Designed as a campus within a single complex building, it was completed and opened in 1965.

A few years later the pressure point reached the level of higher education. After World War II, when a wave of veterans flooded the University of British Columbia, shacks were built — as they had been in the Great War — to accommodate what was thought to be a temporary influx. The demand did not in fact decrease, and in 1960 I taught classes in the same derelict "temporary" buildings that had been put up for the men and women who returned from the war. Before the end of the 1950s a building program was set on foot at the University of British Columbia, but when it became evident that more massive changes were needed, the Social Credit government, with its built-in resentment of Vancouver, decided against spending all its money on extending the existing provincial university.

Instead, it created three others. Victoria College (which by 1961 was giving full degrees as a constituent of the University of British Columbia) was in 1963 elevated to the University of Victoria, and a new campus was created at Gordon Head, outside the city. An entirely new establishment, Simon Fraser University, was chartered, also in 1963, and housed in a spectacular complex — designed by Arthur Erickson — on top of Burnaby Mountain; it was opened in 1965. A privately funded

The great expansion of universities in British Columbia began during Norman MacKenzie's presidency of UBC (1944-62), and only after his retirement were rival universities created.

Conventionally modern in style, the new University of Victoria had little of the architectural innovativeness of Simon Fraser.

In spite of the creation of rivals, the University
of British Columbia also expanded, and its
campus became a mixture of traditional and
modern buildings.

Catholic college at Nelson was at the same time temporarily elevated as Notre Dame University. During the following years a number of regional two-year colleges were established at centres throughout the province to complete the decentralized higher educational system.

In a less formal way, the same period witnessed other significant cultural developments. A revival of the arts manifested itself, not only in painting, writing, and music but especially in the re-emergence of drama as a live art in many parts of the province and the creation of theatres to accommodate it.

The series of centennials — of British Columbia in 1958, of Confederation in 1967, and of British Columbia's entry into the dominion in 1971 — led to a revival of interest in local history and to the appearance of regional museums, of which the most spectacular (the new Provincial Museum in Victoria and the Anthropological Museum in Vancouver) were devoted to giving for the first time an adequate local display of the great arts of the Coast Indians, now appreciated as they had never been before.

The only medical school in B.C. is still at the University of British Columbia, and much extension has gone on in this area, including the Woodward Library and the Woodward Instructional Resources Centre which form the focal point for the sciences linked with health.

For many years the province's rich collection of Coast Indian art was kept in small dark rooms in the basement of the Parliament Buildings. The concern for the past that emerged in the 1960s led to the building of the new Provincial Museum in Victoria.

More recently, in 1977, the University of British Columbia's collection of native arts was housed in the Erickson-designed Museum of Anthropology.

# Ways of Life in the 1970s

I came to British Columbia at the end of the 1940s, and now, as I write at the end of the 1970s, I see a tough continuity in the presence of great change. The look of the cities has been changed by highrises and shopping plazas. The look of the countryside has been changed by dams and roads and the spread of suburbia. The population has more than doubled, and its ethnic mix has altered with every successive wave of immigrants.

First, just after World War II, came the British, largely professionals and technicians. Next came the Dutch, largely market gardeners and nurserymen. They were followed by the Germans who were the first, after the Chinese, to create a distinctive ethnic quarter of Vancouver when they colonized Robson Street into Robsonstrasse. Mediterranean races followed — the Italians and then the Portuguese and the Greeks. Progressively, changes in the immigration laws removed former barriers to Asian immigration, and the number of Chinese, Japanese, and East Indians — mainly Sikhs — resident in British Columbia has notably increased. Today there are 80,000 Chinese in the Greater Vancouver area alone. Successive international disasters have brought their contingents of refugees, from the Hungarians of 1956, through the Czechs and the Tibetans, to the Indochinese of 1979 and the Cubans of 1980.

All these groups have contributed to enrich the artistic and other aspects of the province's cultural life. They have brought new secondary industries; they have introduced new patterns of eating and drinking, and a vast array of exotic restaurants. They have created new leisure patterns.

Yet, for all that, the basic ways of living among British Columbians are surprisingly unchanged. The province remains a region where space and mobility are important to life, where the peculiar conjunction of mountain and sea, of forest and valley, not only infuses the mental life of its people but also dominates their material existence. Secondary industries still play a minor role. The great primary industries of farming and fishing, of mining and smelting, of logging and pulpmaking, of oil and natural gas, still dominate the economy and directly or indirectly dominate the occupational patterns of most British Columbians.

Techniques may change, from handsaws to power saws, from steam to diesel; new crops like grapes may become important and lead to new industries like wine-making. But, essentially, British Columbia still exists by the natural riches of its land and sea, and the ways of life its people follow are bound to these primal realities. The wilderness, eroded though it may be, is still a reality in our lives; the forest reclaims abandoned farms, and wild animals forage on the verges of our cities. To go north is still a way to prove oneself.

Driving cattle in the interior drylands.

Chinese truck farm workers on Lulu Island.

Gathering fruit in the Okanagan.

Unloading herring at Prince Edward.

Operating a giant drill at the Sullivan Mine.

A faller gets away in time!

Self-dumping log barge.

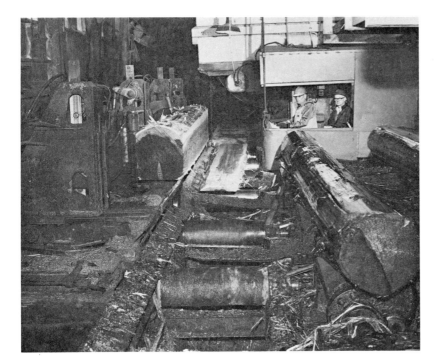

Mechanized sawmill operation.

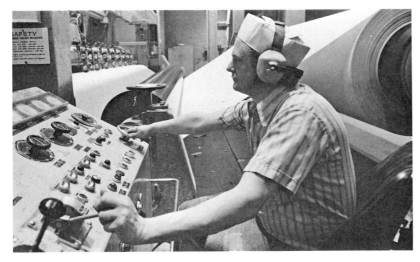

The papermaker.

Loading lumber at North Vancouver.

## Cities Among the Mountains and Sea Channels

British Columbia's spectacular landscape and the abundance of its natural resources have conspired to produce a rapid urbanization. Its broken terrain has meant that it is unfitted for the kind of extensive agriculture that sustained large rural populations in other parts of Canada, so that the relatively small settlements required for industries like mining, fishing, and logging became subsidiary to the coastal cities through which transport was funnelled and in which government, trade, and secondary industry have been concentrated.

The result history has brought is the spectacular growth of one metropolitan centre, Vancouver, the somewhat less rapid growth of a governmental centre, Victoria, and the emergence of a score or so of much smaller regional urban nuclei. There has never been enough level space for the kind of close network of towns that occurs in a region like southern Ontario.

Born in 1886, Vancouver had spread by the 1971 census to bring into a continuous urban pattern other communities like New Westminster and the municipalities north of Burrard Inlet.

Even the mountainous terrain that surrounds it has not halted the growth of Vancouver. From Stanley Park, under the Lion's Gate Bridge, the modern suburbs of West Vancouver can be seen climbing far up the mountainside.

The conventional buildings of an earlier
Vancouver are being replaced by modern
towers of glass and concrete and steel
(upper left). Some of the streets that pass
among the towers have been turned into malls
where no traffic but buses is allowed
(lower left).

In Victoria, developments like the Centennial
Square with its modernist fountain
(upper right) and the McPherson Theatre,
designed for live stage productions
(lower right), illustrate a general trend to
change the face of British Columbian cities.

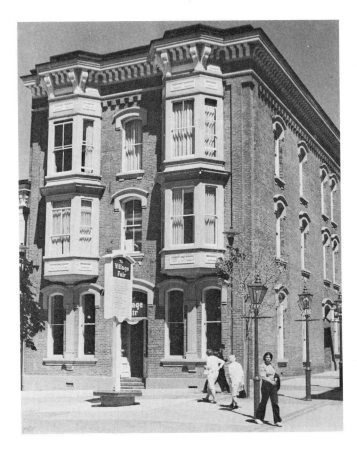

As well as constructing new buildings, architects have been rediscovering and putting to new uses some fine old ones. The Village Fair in Victoria occupies the handsome 1860s hotel, Burnes House in Bastion Square (above left); and the Art Gallery of Greater Victoria utilizes a large Victorian mansion that from 1899 to 1903 was the lieutenant governor's official residence (above right).

As Greater Vancouver, it has become the third city of Canada, the nation's leading seaport, and the leading city of the rapidly growing West, with a population of 1,082,000, approximately 50 per cent of the total population of British Columbia. It has now all the major features of a large modern city, made unique by the close proximity of both mountains and ocean. These, together with a temperate climate that sometimes offers year-round golfing, have encouraged a hedonistic way of life that has led envious central Canadians to describe British Columbia as the authentic Land of the Lotus Eaters.

Victoria has never recovered the start as the province's principal city which it lost to Vancouver by the early 1890s. Although it remains the capital city and has recovered from the stagnation of the depression era, it still lags far behind in numbers and wealth. The population of Greater Victoria in 1971 was approximately 196,000, or about 9 per cent of the province's population of 2,184,000. Approximately another 11 per cent of the province's population lived in seventeen communities of more than 5,000 each, meaning that 70 per cent of British Columbians at the beginning of the 1970s were urban dwellers, even though no province of Canada was more dependent on the natural resources of its hinterland. But it is significant of the high degree of concentration British Columbian trade and industries have attained that none of the cities other than Victoria has more than 3 per cent of Greater Vancouver's population. The largest

There still remain dark corners of the cities, like Fan Tan Alley in Victoria's Chinatown (above left), and frontier communities that have vegetated, like the decaying mining town of Wells (above right) in the Cariboo.

The Lotus Land that outsiders see in British Columbia is the product of a relatively mild environment and a varied terrain that allows a wide range of leisure activities. Dancers perform out of doors in downtown Vancouver.

In English Bay, boats sail against the backdrop of Vancouver's highrises.

in 1971 were Prince George in the northern interior with 33,000 people, Kamloops with 26,000, and Port Alberni with 20,000.

This has meant that the styles of building in Vancouver are more lavish and grandiose than elsewhere in the province and that styles of living are more cosmopolitan, influenced alike by Europe, the Orient, and Latin America, to all of which the city is directly linked by CP Air and other airlines.

Victoria still retains its hybrid English and Pacific Coast flavour, and the lesser towns remain largely dominated by their particular economic interests — fishing in Prince Rupert, fruit growing in Kelowna, paper and pulp in Prince George, ranching in Kamloops — and sometimes by special ethnic combinations, like those induced by the presence of a large Italian community in Trail, of Mennonites of German descent in the towns of the lower Fraser Valley, of Russian-speaking Doukhobors in Nelson and Grand Forks. With its ethnic quarters and its terrain broken by salt- and fresh-water channels, Vancouver of course reproduces this variety on a metropolitan scale and thus perpetuates the original gold-rush life view that British Columbians, native or adoptive, have never quite forgotten — the sense of a flexible, expandable community with an open future.

On mountains like Big White in the
Okanagan, skiing continues for long seasons.

In the interior, the lake fronts — like that of
Kelowna — are places of summer idling.

Many touches suggest the multicultural origins of British Columbia's peoples, like the Buddhist temple in Japanese style at Steveston (left) and a restaurant in Tyrolean manner in Victoria (above).

# Moving into the Eighties

By 1972 the social democrats, whether CCF or NDP, had been the province's second party for so long that at times it seemed they would ossify into a permanent opposition. Their coming to power was largely through the personal vigour of Dave Barrett, who did not allow his socialist theorizing to blind him to the fact that W. A. C. Bennett had held power for twenty years through a masterly manipulation of multiple interests. Barrett realized that the NDP would never be elected as a party representing only labour interests. He was not popular with the local labour bosses, and this liberated him to woo other groups, like teachers, intellectuals, even merchants. He took over Bennett's populist stance and insisted that the NDP was the party not of one class but of the people in general.

Like Bennett before him, Barrett was also a loner who made a virtue of being badly treated by the establishment. In 1959 he was sacked from his post in the provincial prisons service because he ran for election as a CCF candidate. In 1969 he was

Dave Barrett brought an end in 1972 to the longest premiership in British Columbian history when he ended W. A. C. Bennett's twenty-year period of office and formed the province's first social democratic government. It remained in office from 1972 to 1975.

The polarization of British Columbian politics that in recent years has meant the alternation of NDP and Social Credit governments is rooted in the deep conflicts which emerge in a society heavily dominated by industries exploiting natural resources. Such industries create militancy among the workers, leading to a strong socialist movement with its roots in places like the smelting town of Trail (above), the fishing port of Prince Rupert (left), and the many communities that in one way or another are dominated by the timber industry.

On British Columbian cities of the 1970s Arthur Erickson made the same kind of mark as Maclure and Rattenbury did in earlier decades. His MacMillan Bloedel Building on Georgia Street in Vancouver has made its own severe contribution to the highrise profile of the city.

beaten in a bid for leadership of the NDP because the labour bosses put their votes behind his rival, Tom Berger. But Berger lost the 1969 election, and in 1970 Barrett became leader in his place. He owed nothing to the unions or to much more than his own personality and vigour, and these qualities appealed — as they had with Bennett in his younger days — to the British Columbian electorate.

Barrett's victory was so spectacular a reversal of political fortunes that, with his large majority, great changes were expected. In fact, he carried out a series of welcome reforms, such as making the legal system and the welfare system more humane and stopping the sale of farmlands to developers. But in terms of socializing services and industries, his record was less than spectacular. His threats to take over the British Columbia Telephone Company never materialized. His takeover of automobile insurance and his acquisition of a couple of pulp mill operations, due for abandonment by their owners, compared poorly with Bennett's expropriation of the giant British Columbia Electric Company and his creation of a provincial bank and a provincial ferry service.

But the enemies he made rather than his failure to bring socialism to British Columbia proved Barrett's undoing. He alienated university and school teachers as well as parents by erratic educational budgeting based on untested theories. He angered the unions by legislating an end to three major strikes at once, on the grounds that the interests of the people as a whole had precedence over those of labour. And he angered everyone else by doubling MLAs' salaries and raising his own to $52,000 — $4,000 more than the prime minister of Canada then received.

Barrett gave his opposition the weapons to use against him, and they did not hesitate to fight bitterly in a contest that showed more clearly than ever the extent to which provincial politics had become polarized outside the old party systems. Almost all the leaders of the provincial Liberals and Tories joined the Social Credit party, leaving their organizations decimated and demoralized. The result of this consolidated antisocialist front was a turning of tables like that of 1972. In the 1975 election the NDP was reduced to seventeen seats and Social Credit, led by Bill Bennett, son of the former premier, gained thirty-seven seats.

Since 1975, Social Credit has remained in power in Victoria. It has been a much more austere regime than the Social Credit government of the 1950s and 1960s. The elder Bennett held office in a period of almost continuous expansion, and so he could rule by gifts. Recognizing the situation, Bill Bennett began with a group of unpopular measures, such as doubling ferry rates and raising automobile insurance premiums to balance the budget. More recently, he has begun to offer gifts — reductions in provincial and municipal taxes, a dental plan, and, most imaginative, the mass privatization of the British Columbia

Yet in his courthouse complex, housing provincial government offices, Erickson challenges the pattern of glass and concrete towers by opening the centre of the city to a harmonious multilevelled area of offices, gardens, and leisure spaces.

Erickson's Sikh Temple, overlooking the Fraser River, is a remarkable evocation of the spirit of Asian austerity in a modern western idiom.

After his father's defeat in 1972 and retirement from active politics, Bill Bennett had to fight a hard internal battle against older party stalwarts before he finally inherited the Social Credit party leadership and was able to guide the party toward the electoral victory that brought it back to power in 1975.

Resources Investment Corporation (which runs the enterprises taken over by the NDP government) by giving shares to every man, woman, and child in the province. The BCRIC is now being used to keep ownership of British Columbian resources out of alien hands; it has just become major shareholder in the great forest firm of MacMillan Bloedel and second shareholder in the Kaiser enterprise that dominates coal mining in the East Kootenays.

The polarization of politics within British Columbia has been paralleled by a somewhat different polarization of federal politics. Provincially divided between Social Credit and NDP, voters tend to be federally divided between Conservative and NDP. Only one Liberal was elected in the province in 1979, and none in 1980. British Columbian federal Conservatism is not an expression of separatism, which at present is a minor trend in the province, but of a deep discontent with the administrative centralization associated with the Liberal government and the tendency for federal politics to be governed by eastern Canadian problems — and especially the problem of Quebec, which British Columbians feel has too obsessively dominated national affairs.

The average British Columbian does not at present see himself as other than a Canadian, but he feels that his province's interests and its contribution to the country are alike largely ignored in the centralist interpretation that Ottawa has given to Canadian federalism in recent years.

Bill Bennett's stronghold, like his father's, is the sunny orchard-surrounded town of Kelowna in the deep interior of British Columbia. Okanagan Lake faces it like a great moat crossed by a long causeway and bridge.

Towns like Kelowna, and like Nelson shown in this photograph, provide the unchanging small-town conservatism on which Social Credit has always depended for the basis of its support.

In places like Erickson's Robson Square in Vancouver, European influences and architectural styles developed within British Columbia combine to define the special way of life, highly regional and at the same time cosmopolitan, which British Columbians feel is their unique contribution to Canada.

233

# Index

# Picture Credits

The principal sources of prints are identified by the abbreviations given below. We would like to thank the individuals and the staffs of institutions involved for their co-operation in providing illustrative material. In case any source has been inadvertently overlooked, we apologize and would appreciate being informed of this so that acknowledgement can be made in a later edition.

| | |
|---|---|
| BCFS | British Columbia Forest Service |
| BCH | British Columbia Hydro & Power Authority |
| CPA | Canadian Pacific Airlines |
| CPR | Canadian Pacific Railway |
| CVA | City of Vancouver Archives |
| EA | Eaton's Archives |
| GF | Glenbow Foundation |
| HBC | Hudson's Bay Company |
| IW | Ingeborg Woodcock |
| IW & SN | Ingeborg Woodcock and Sono Nis Press |
| MB | MacMillan Bloedel |
| MTLB | Metropolitan Toronto Library Board |
| NGC | National Gallery of Canada |
| NMC | National Museums of Canada |
| NMM | National Maritime Museum, Greenwich, England |
| PABC | Public Archives of British Columbia |
| PAC | Public Archives of Canada |
| PC | Private collections of books and periodicals |
| ROM | Royal Ontario Museum |
| TBC | Tourism British Columbia |
| UBC | University of British Columbia, Special Collections |
| VCM | Vancouver Centennial Museum |

**p.8,** CPR, MB; **p.9,** BCH, IW; **p.10,** NMC, PC; **p.11,** IW, PAC 17760; **p.12,** UBC, PAC C-17726; **p.13,** PC, NMM; **p.14,** VCM, PAC C-2821; **p.15,** VCM, PABC 7949, PABC 3591; **p.16,** PC, PC; **p.17,** PAC C-12267, PABC 12459, PABC 7408; **p.18,** HBC; **p.19,** NGC, HBC; **p.20,** PABC 28148, PABC 27778; **p.21,** PABC 10230, GF 1638; **p.22,** ROM 921-1-97, PABC 127; **p.23,** PABC 755, NMC; **p.24,** GF 8438, PAC C-34089, HBC; **p.25,** ROM 912-1-84, ROM 912-1-91; **p.26,** ROM 912-1-93, PABC 2656; **p.27,** HBC; **p.28,** PABC 33188(a), PABC 2656; **p.29,** IW & SN, PAC 11040; **p.30,** IW & SN, MTLB; **p.31,** MTLB, PAC C-9561; **p.32,** PABC 3495, PABC 3493; **p.33,** PABC 7756; **p.34,** PABC 5136, PABC 4578; **p.35,** PC, PC, PAC C-34095; **p.36,** PABC 28446; **p.37,** GF 491, PABC 1906, IW & SN; **p.38,** PABC 4967; **p.39,** PABC 23094; **p.40,** IW & SN; **p.41,** PABC 17310, PABC 28433, PAC C-23401; **p.42,** PABC 25397, PABC; **p.43,** PC; **p.44,** PABC 28243, PC, PC; **p.45,** PABC 717; **p.46,** PABC 24288, PABC 9324(c); **p.47,** PC, PC, PABC 39180; **p.48,** ROM 962-100-4, ROM 950-9-17; **p.49,** PABC 231; **p.50,** IW & SN, NMM, PC; **p.51,** NMM; **p.52,** NMM; **p.53,** PABC 28232, PABC 13189; **p.54,** NMM, PAC C-26480; **p.55,** PABC 28210, PABC 28244; **p.56,** PC, PABC 2526; **p.57,** PABC 91727, PABC 28234, PC; **p.58,** Confederation Life, PABC 10228; **p.59,** PABC 763, PABC 56378; **p.60,** PABC 9565, PABC 12245, PABC 51730; **p.61,** PABC 3290, PAC C-9583; **p.62,** PAC 9588, PABC 7106; **p.63,** McCord Museum M-466; **p.64,** PC; **p.65,** PC; **p.66,** PABC 1232; **p.67,** PABC 2438, PC; **p.68,** PC, PABC 90266; **p.69,** MTLB; **p.70,** PABC 809; **p.71,** PABC 8941, IW; **p.72,** PABC 52177, PABC 10501; **p.73,** PABC 10497, PABC 81499; **p.74,** PAC C-36082, PAC C-36108; **p.75,** PC, PABC 2979; **p.76,** PAC 35986, PABC 12682; **p.77,** PAC 36107, PAC 27; **p.78,** PAC C-294; **p.79,** PABC 7749, PAC 136103; **p.80,** PABC 2419, PAC PA-14201; **p.81,** PABC 3044, PABC 3369; **p.82,**

PAC C-107375, PC; **p.83**, IW & SN, PC, PABC 84; **p.84**, IW, EA; **p.85**, PC, PABC 2716; **p.86**, PAC C-3854, PAC C-37841; **p.87**, MTLB; **p.88**, PABC 66243, PC; **p.89**, GF 1730, PAC C-23226; **p.90**, PC, PABC 2705, PAC C-35936; **p.91**, PC, PABC 49564; **p.92**, PAC PA-25030, PAC PA-9138; **p.93**, PAC PA-51137; **p.94**, PAC PA-22618; **p.95**, PAC C-7656, PAC C-8549, PABC 2917; **p.96**, GF NA-782-6; **p.97**, PAC C-2824, PC; **p.98**, PC; **p.99**, PABC 42356, CPR; **p.100**, PABC 13167, PABC 73337; **p.101**, CVA, PABC 6759; **p.102**, PABC 82704; **p.103**, PABC 1187, PABC 7305; **p.104**, HBC, HBC; **p.105**, ROM 912-1-60; **p.106**, PAC C-1573, NGC; **p.107**, NGC; **p.108**, PC; **p.109**, GF 6158, GF 342; **p.110**, NGC & Vancouver Art Gallery; **p.111**, VCM, ROM 912-1-87, PABC 28276; **p.112**, IW, GF 4674; **p.113**, PABC 66699; **p.114**, UBC, NMC; **p.115**, PABC 46690; **p.116**, PAC C-14099; **p.117**, PABC 23081, PC; **p.118**, PAC C-33996, PABC 43512; **p.119**, IW, PABC 2718; **p.120**, PABC 67644; **p.121**, PAC C-21987; **p.122**, PABC 42709, PABC 67646; **p.123**, PABC 31705, PABC 11323; **p.124**, IW; **p.125**, CVA; **p.126**, PABC 45902; **p.127**, PABC 5235; **p.128**, PABC 40582; **p.129**, PABC 53243, PABC 45091; **p.130**, Cominco; **p.132**, PABC 36631; **p.133**, PABC 8090; **p.134**, PABC 2696, PC; **p.135**, IW, PABC 27426; **p.136**, PC; **p.137**, GF 272, PABC 11581; **p.138**, PA 22548; **p.140**, PABC 10233; **p.141**, PABC 1067; **p.142**, IW & SN, PC, GF 1993; **p.143**, PABC 353, PABC 29365; **p.144**, PC, CVA; **p.145**, PABC 75209, PABC 10464; **p.146**, National Museum of Science and Technology, CVA; **p.148**, CVA, PABC 4580; **p.149**, PABC 31553, PABC 13160; **p.150**, PABC 12040, PABC 51747; **p.151**, PAC C-20932, PABC 43680; **p.152**, PC; **p.153**, PAC C-4677, PABC 67870; **p.154**, PAC PA-11590, PABC 23687; **p.156**, PABC 36762, IW & SN; **p.157**, BCH, CPR; **p.158**, CVA; **p.159**, IW, HBC; **p.160**, PABC 8760, PABC 12931; **p.161**, PABC 25598, United Church Archives; **p.162**, PABC 29495; **p.163**, HBC, PABC 27472; **p.164**, PABC 8336; **p.165**, IW & SN, PABC 68631; **p.166**, PAC, PABC 63689; **p.167**, CVA; **p.168**, CVA; **p.169**, CVA; **p.170**, IW & SN; **p.171**, PC; **p.172**, UBC, IW & SN; **p.174**, CPR; **p.175**, HBC; **p.176**, HBC, HBC; **p.177**, PABC 65853; **p.178**, BCH; **p.179**, IW & SN; **p.180**, TBC; **p.181**, PABC 6750, PABC 2518; **p.182**, PABC 42519, TBC; **p.183**, TBC, TBC; **p.184**, PABC 67840, PABC 67849; **p.185**, PABC 67830; **p.186**, PAC C-27901; **p.187**, PABC 82089; **p.188**, PABC 16484, PABC 93039; **p.189**, TBC; **p.190**, PAC C-29399, PAC C-27900; **p.191**, PAC 20596, PAC C-74967; **p.192**, CVA & Vancouver Province; **p.193**, IW & SN, PAC DND-Navy-E-139; **p.194**, CPR; **p.195**, MB, Westcoast Transmission; **p.196**, Cominco, **p.197**, Cominco, Cominco; **p.198**, CPA, CPA; **p.199**, Alcan; **p.200**, PABC 64718; **p.201**, Alcan, Westcoast Transmission; **p.202**, PABC 71976; **p.203**, TBC; **p.204**, TBC, BCH; **p.205**, BCH, BCH; **p.206**, TBC, CPR; **p.207**, PABC; **p.208**, EA; **p.209**, IW & SN, UBC; **p.210**, UBC; **p.211**, UBC; **p.212**, TBC, UBC; **p.214**, TBC, IW; **p.215**, TBC, TBC, Cominco; **p.216**, BCFS, MB; **p.217**, MB, MB, BCFS; **p.218**, TBC; **p.219**, EA, BCH; **p.220**, IW & SN, IW & SN; **p.221**, IW & SN; **p.222**, IW & SN, IW, EA; **p.223**, TBC; **p.224**, TBC, TBC; **p.225**, IW & SN, IW; **p.226**, New Democratic Party of British Columbia; **p.227**, TBC, TBC; **p.228**, EA; **p.229**, EA, EA; **p.230**, Social Credit Party of British Columbia, TBC; **p.231**, TBC; **p.232**, EA.

**Edited by Carlotta Lemieux**
**Designed by David Shaw**
**Composed by Pickering Type House**
**Manufactured by T. H. Best Company Ltd.**